F. Pérez Lopez's
El Mexicano

F. Pérez Lopez's
El Mexicano

※◒◓◒※

a retelling by
Gary Soto

STEPHEN F. AUSTIN STATE UNIVERSITY PRESS

For more information:
Stephen F. Austin State University Press
P.O. Box 13007 SFA Station
Nacogdoches, Texas 75962
sfapress@sfasu.edu
www.sfasu.edu/sfapress

Book design: Tanner O'Neal. Joshua J. Hines
Distrubted by Texas A&M Consortium
www.tamupress.com

First Edition
ISBN: 978-1-62288-163-5

Acknowledgments

Francisco Pérez López's Le Mexicain was published in France in 1970 by Robert Lafont. The English translation, Dark and Bloody Ground, was published in 1972 by Little, Brown and Company. The current publisher of Le Mexicain is La Manufacture de livre of France. Gary Soto drew from the US edition of Dark and Bloody Ground but used wholly new language in his retelling.

Permission requests regarding the book in hand should be directed to Stephen F. Austin State University Press. Inquiries for film or publication of Pérez López's original book should be directed to Pierre Fourniaud at La Manufacture de livre of France.

The untitled cover photo is from Southworth Spanish Civil War Collection housed in Special Collections at the University of California at San Diego. Used by permission.

This retelling was written in spring 2017, the 100th anniversary of Francisco Pérez López's birth. The author wishes to thank Peter Fong and Carolyn Soto for their editorial suggestions. He also wishes to thank Pierre Fourniaud for permission to retell this story.

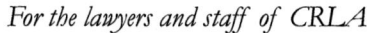

For the lawyers and staff of CRLA

Beginnings

At one point during the Spanish Civil War, a platoon within the Garibaldi Battalion of the International Brigades included a Czech, a Cuban, a Mexican, four Italians, three Frenchmen, several Englishmen, two Finns, an American, a Dutchman, an Irishman and a wayward Catalan youth. Their signature hats: berets. Their purpose: to fight for the rightfully elected government of Manuel Azaña, a left-leaning president, against the ideologically conservative Nationalist factions lead by General Francisco Franco. Their target: sneak attacks along the Ebro River and the cliffs and summits of Sierra de Caballs and Sierra de Pandols. This was 1938, with the war near its conclusion.

My interest in the platoon concerns a farmworker's diary, each page filled from top to bottom, the sentences written without punctuation or paragraph breaks. It involves a chance meeting between that farmworker and a scholar while the two smoked cigarettes one evening in 1967. The result of this meeting? *Le Mexicain,* a memoir published in France in 1970. In its simplicity the reader discovers truth stripped to its essence. There is no showmanship in the prose, little in the way of reflection, absolutely no conclusion. The cause is supreme.

Subtitled "A Guerrilla Diary of the Spanish Civil War," the book was also published as *Dark and Bloody Ground* in the United States in 1972 and received one modest printing. The author and farmworker was Francisco Pérez Lopez. Here's how it was written. The young scholar, Victor Guerrier, was engaged in historical research on the French Revolution at a chateau in the village of Haute-Provence, France. The chateau's owners permitted Guerrier to use the library at their residence and, because his research began in winter, a village woman would arrive daily to make the fire. The two would sometimes have coffee together. Soon the scholar was introduced to the villager's husband, Francisco, then in his early fifties but still lean, with a brisk stride. A cordial friend-ship from the start.

One evening, after Guerrier had explained the exasperations of his book project, Pérez Lopez casually mentioned that he was writing a book as well.

A book? Really?

To Victor, Francisco was a farmworker, not a writer, though with pad and pencil he was a compulsive chronicler of daily farm tasks. What was his book? Francisco disappeared then soon re-turned with several large notebooks. Victor sat up. The unpoetic working title was "A study of the political affair in Spain, as seen by Francisco Pérez Lopez, undated, but told according to reality."

Thus Francisco shared his diary for the first time—even his wife had known nothing of his private project. His writing, Victor discovered, was devoid of sentimentality. His narrative consisted of declarative facts with no afterthoughts. Francisco's efforts to document the war began with dates, people, and places—written on cigarette paper while he was in prison. The diary begins with his childhood.

Francisco was born in Spain in 1916 and raised in Arles, France, by his mother and grandmother, his father and grand-father having died within months of each other of the Spanish flu. During childhood, Francisco governed his own comings and goings. He grew up at a time when the world was quiet—even ra-dios were not then common. Like most male youth, he had a pen-chant for football, flirted with girls, occasionally attended Catholic service and, above all, spent afternoons with friends, discussing matters of importance at their age.

Francisco attended school until age fourteen, after which he enrolled in trade school, where he was adept at woodworking and carpentry. But he quickly grew bored and quit his apprenticeship. In his late teens he worked as a fisherman, smuggled black-mar-ket goods, and got a job as an extra in a traveling circus. At a notoriously rough bar, he was hired as a lookout while clandestine activities went on in the cellar. With his grandmother he sailed to Algeria, where his rich grand-uncles maintained tracts of farm-land, always to the detriment of the workers. There he saw for the first time one of the typical uses of economic power: stingy men who become wealthy by the other people's labor. His cynical Uncle Antonio summed up his status as *patron* like this: "I provide food for them and they make me rich." Francisco was appalled.

In Arles, Francisco watched as men arrived from the four cor-ners of the world to fight for the Spanish Republic against Franco and fascism. He was moved by the physical power displayed by the youthful soldiers and intrigued by their dedication to a cause. What cause did he embrace? What higher meaning? At that point, he had just kicked about in life.

Then an incident occurred: "One morning at four there was a loud knocking on the door: the police, tommy guns in hand." Francisco was escorted from his room, interrogated at a police station, shoved and prodded, spat upon, punched and—when he has answered their questions honestly—punched again. He was jailed for four days as a suspect in the murder of a gendarme at a border crossing. When the police eventually released him, they offered only excuses and little smiles—sorry, you're the wrong person. The murderer has already been caught. The murderer has been dealt with.

This was the tipping point.

Regarding his collaboration with Francisco during the time before publication, Victor Guerrier observed: "But if I tried to make him develop the 'interesting' moments of the narrative, he would swerve away." Francisco refused to embellish an event; in-stead, he told it as objectively as a police report. Once a death on the battlefield had been recorded, there was for him no sense in pondering its bloody significance. The dead around Francis-co were just that: dead. As platoon leader, prisoner and escapee, his mind looked forward. Only what lay ahead—behind a tree or boulder, in vineyards or fig groves, in a pile of snow, among a set of houses or down the steps of a cellar—was worth his furtive attention. Pausing to contemplate past actions could lead to further casualties. This he learned from the beginning.

Francisco's life is unrepeatable in its stoicism and extraordinary purpose, and dramatic beyond one's imagination. He is driven by a sense of justice. In dealing with the enemy, there is no diplomacy or mercy. Here skirmishes and battles, the wounds and the deaths, are tallied from the beginning of his involvement in the Spanish Civil War in 1938 until his march into France near the end of 1941. Here is an abbreviation of his diary.

With the Commando Unit of the XV International Brigade

In mid-March 1938 Francisco arrives by train in Barcelona. He is not more than a few yards from the station when sirens sound. Minutes later the ground shakes from bombs released from the planes of Franco's Nationalist Army—modern planes supplied by Nazi Germany. He descends into a tunnel and waits until the bombing ceases. By happenstance, an official of the Republican Army is seated there at a small table. Francisco shows this official his identification papers. A day later he is sent to the Recruits Barracks. An officer provides him with a ration card that says *Permiso d'Estado Mayor*. With this card, he can seek a meal at any barracks within Barcelona. He also is given documents that allow him to draw pocket money.

Francisco passes his medical exam and pleases a captain during his obligatory interview. As a new arrival unfamiliar with the city, he spends most of his time meandering through barrios, sitting in cafés, and going to the movies. He is often on the beach, where he watches boats arrive with their haul—the sardines are grilled in pits on the beach. He frequents a nightclub in an area called Barrio Chino. He is a young man with time on his hands.

One morning at roll call, he is asked to step forward. The waiting is over. Francisco is one of about three hundred volunteers who will train to become soldiers. During the next few weeks, he receives lessons on military etiquette and combat. He practices the use of a dagger in close combat, learns how to locate landmines, and repeatedly breaks down and reassembles his rifle. He takes target practice and becomes acquainted with the tommy gun, which will become his weapon of choice. He pals around nightly with his new comrades. After a month, he is given a new khaki uniform along with two pairs of socks, a pair of new shoes and a cap with a red pompom. He is assigned to 1st Company, XV International Brigade, 1st Death Platoon, 35th Division, with no apparent rank. His insignia is a skull with crossbones. Later he learns that the patches of this insignia are given to those soldiers to be deployed in larger battles.

He briefly bunks at the Karl Marx Barracks, then he and other recruits board a train. At each stop locals present the volunteers with flowers and baskets of fruit. Some recruits get off, others stay on. After a few hours on the train, Francisco disembarks to spend the evening at a mansion set in an apple orchard.

At daybreak the recruits again board a train. They disembark at Olot, a town near the French border, receive a box of supplies, including eating utensils and another uniform, then are taken to a church in a little village called Las Presas. During roll call, Francisco learns that he will stay at a nearby farm. He is heartily welcomed by the farmer, who treats him like a son and feeds him until he can no longer eat. The farmer and his wife have two daughters, ages twenty-five and twenty-one. The one named Amelia has her eye on Francisco. There are also female nurses waiting to be called to the front.

The next day a truck rolls up and out jump fifteen soldiers, all with the same insignia stitched on their sleeves. They are from different countries, but most speak at least some French. The men are Dutch, Swiss, French, Finnish, English, Mexican, Cuban, German, Polish, Belgian, Irish, American, and Czech—and all are backing the Republican cause against Franco's fascists. That evening they eat outdoors at a long table, drink as young men will drink, sing songs, and share stories. All the volunteers are full of talk except the Czech, who is reluctant to share his personal history.

The captain of the Christopher Columbus Barracks announces that the platoon is now part of the Garibaldi Battalion. He appoints Francisco platoon leader because he can speak and write in both French and Spanish. His new rank is sergeant. The names of the soldiers under his command include Hirmand, Van Derart, Hotto, Picard, Jones, Vallier, and, to Francisco's ear, foreign-sounding "Tommie." The captain distributes new arms, daggers, maps, a radio transmitter and manuals on battlefield strategy. The volunteers remain at the farm for a month, studying maps, drilling and practicing guerilla tactics. They learn to lay landmines and dynamite. And they fatten up for the coming battles.

Reconnaissance Operations on the Ebro

On April 14th the Garibaldi Battalion is trucked day and night to an undisclosed military front. They stop at a village destroyed by bombs—not a single inhabitant remains. Only abandoned goats, chickens, and pigs greet them. They hike two miles into the hills, their supplies on the backs of donkeys. They establish headquarters in an abandoned convent, where they find canisters of olive oil, sacks of rice and beans, and jugs of wine free for the taking. In the overgrown gardens, they glean potatoes, onions, and tomatoes.

Alone, Francisco climbs a nearby hill. On the other side of the river is the enemy—he can hear rifle shots and the sounds of what he believes are tanks. The situation does not strike Francisco as dangerous, though he worries that the volunteers are too few if the enemy should cross the river and attack. He returns to camp, worried yet not worried.

They stay at the convent for three weeks, then are ordered

to move into a position above the Ebro. They can hear the enemy's voices in conversation on the other side of the river, along with the rhythms of Moroccan drumming, which they sometimes enjoy. Crouching behind trees and thickets, they scrutinize the enemy's movements. To Francisco, the enemy soldiers appear to be easy targets, but he does not have the authority to call for an attack. One evening the platoon encounters two defectors: a staff doctor and a sergeant. Both openly offer information on the Nationalist Army and its maneuvers.

Francisco's platoon is ordered to engage in random skirmishes. For a week they go out each night, killing lax sentries stationed at bridges or squads of soldiers on patrol. They take no prisoners, even those who raise their hands in surrender. This becomes the norm, which sits well with Francisco. He is aware that if he or any of the Republican soldiers surrender in battle they are usually executed on the spot. And when a volunteer of the International Brigades is caught by Franco's Moroccan soldiers, his head is lopped off and sometimes stuck on a pole for villagers to see.

The conflicts become more intense. One night the platoon raids an enemy camp positioned above the Ebro. They come upon two sentries and stab them to death, but their cries waken the other Moroccans asleep around small campfires. Francisco's platoon uses tommy guns, rifles, and daggers to kill the remaining soldiers, fifty or more. The platoon collects some of their weapons then scampers away to set up a line of defense on the beach.

When the counterattack begins, mortar shells fall around them. Machine guns rattle, then stop. There's a pause before the enemy—army regulars, Carlists, Legionnaires, Civil Guardsmen and Moroccans—begin to charge across the river. The platoon fires at will. Francisco alone kills twenty-seven within the span of an hour. One American volunteer is hit in the shoulder. Otherwise, the platoon is unscathed.

When a lookout reports an enemy column on the move, the platoon abandons its position on the beach and takes cover in the brush on higher ground. Francisco hears war chants before the enemy appears, rifles waving jubilantly above their heads as they begin to cross the shallow river. Francisco counts perhaps three hundred Moroccans, mistakenly celebrating the end of the skirmish. They continue to chant and dance, moving closer and closer. When they're not more than twenty yards away, Francisco's two machine guns begin to fire. The enemy falls in numbers, then retreats to their side of the river.

An hour of silence is broken only by an occasional rifle shot. Then the enemy once again begins to cross the river. The platoon fires upon them until the heaps of corpses grow so high that the Moroccans use their dead comrades as walls to enable their attack. Francisco's platoon seems destined for defeat but for the appearance of two Republican tanks. The tanks fire until the Moroccans rise from their positions and begin to scatter. When the shooting is over, the enemy dead and wounded number near six hundred. Francisco says: "You could cross it [the river] without touching the water, it was so full of corpses."

The fighting lasts two hours and twenty-five minutes, according to Francisco's watch. In his platoon one American and one Swiss are killed, while one American and one Belgian are wounded. He himself suffers a sprained ankle.

The platoon returns to the convent. A day later the Nationalist Army retaliates with outdated biplanes that strafe the Republican positions and hurl grenades from open cockpits. The forest around the church burns, and the earth trembles from the pounding of long-range artillery. Inside the convent, plaster rains down and dust fills their clothing like sand. The volunteers wait in the cellar until the bombardment stops.

When the battle is over, Francisco learns that the Republican Army has lost forty men, while the Nationalist Army's casualties approach seven hundred, mostly Moroccans. After three days, the platoon is trucked to Torre de Fontaubella, where they establish a campsite in the countryside. The recuperating battalions include the Garibaldi, the Maptan, and the Lincoln, along with a squadron of Polish Cavalry. Francisco's platoon is filled out with four replacements: an American, two Poles, and a Finn. They are also receive special equipment for tactics in water: rubber pants, nylon rope, and inflatable bags for keeping their weapons dry.

Raid at the Mouth of the Ebro

Francisco's platoon and others are trucked to the province of Tarragona, where they prepare for a raid. After the officers receive their instructions, the volunteers set off, crossing bridges and mountain passes. Each platoon is assigned to a different beachfront along the Ebro. Francisco's platoon positions itself in a cane field. The atmosphere is quiet; only now and then the distant sound of enemy planes causes the volunteers to worry. Although the river is only fifteen yards away, Francisco does not allow his men to refill their canteens. There could be snipers on the other side.

Near midnight the volunteers undress then don their waterproof pants to cross the river. The Finn, a good swimmer, is the first to reach the opposite bank. There he ties a nylon rope to a tree. One by one the men cross the river, an inflatable raft cradling their weapons. On the other side, they dress in the uniforms of Civil Guardsmen and Nationalists Army—"costumes," Francisco calls them. They cross a set of railroad tracks and come upon a lone cottage guarded by sentries. Using hand signals, Francisco instructs two of his soldiers to action. They kill the sentries with daggers.

Francisco approaches the cottage. Its windows are bright from the glow of kerosene lamps, and he can hear laughter and accordion music. He scurries up onto the porch. He jerks open the door and surprises the enemy soldiers. They all surrender except for a major, who fumbles for the pistol in his holster. The Czech kills him with a burst of fire from his tommy gun. The platoon marches its prisoners back to the river and over the bridge. The Republican soldiers stationed there lead the prisoners away.

Not yet done for the night, Francisco and his platoon of volunteers return to the area around the cottage. He and the Dutchman, dressed in Civil Guardsmen uniforms, scale a rocky hill. While stepping over and around some large holes in the rock, they are surprised to find a squad of Carlist soldiers asleep. Because of their uniforms, Francisco and the Dutchman are welcomed by a groggy Carlist. The volunteers drop themselves into the hole and pretend to get comfortable. Francisco makes some excuse to one of the Carlists, and he and the Dutchman climb out. He notes three other holes and quickly signals his platoon to surround them. A few minutes later they toss grenades into the holes. Thirteen enemy soldiers are killed; Francisco allows those who survive to run into the hills.

The platoon is headed back to the river when Francisco stops an enemy supply truck. They set fire to the truck after killing the soldiers, two of whom are from the Italian army—Mussolini is aiding Franco with soldiers and equipment, particularly cannons and outdated planes. As the platoon resumes their rush for the river, an Englishman is killed by a burst of machine-gun fire. They hunker down and wait until they can locate the machine gun by its yellowish flash. Francisco and two of his men surprise and kill the gunner by approaching from behind, and Francisco captures an enemy soldier attempting to escape. When he asks the soldier a question and he answers in Italian, Francisco shoots him on the spot.

The raid has resulted in the death of one volunteer soldier, with another injured. The enemy has lost a major, two captains, seven Carlists, and three Italians. Eleven Nationalist soldiers have been captured, along with a machine gun and twenty-eight grenades, and four cannons destroyed.

The next morning the enemy shells the cane fields with cannons and mortars. Planes strafe the volunteers' positions and bullets whizz above their heads. Angry at the onslaught, the Czech climbs a tree and sets up a machine gun. When he hits a low-flying plane, it spirals upward then straight down into the river, the pilot presumed dead in his cockpit.

In the afternoon Francisco's platoon is relieved by fresh Republican troops. During their time away from the front, the men spend two weeks at the Karl Marx Barracks in Barcelona. Each soldier receives his pay: five thousand pesetas. The platoon washes and repairs their uniforms; they eat, get haircuts, see movies, visit nightclubs; and they also add two recruits, a Mexican and a Cuban. Their bruises and scrapes, their back pains and sore feet, all but disappear. Francisco visits an injured soldier, a Pole, at the Calle Tallere hospital.

On orders the platoon is trucked to the village of Falset, where they camp under hazelnut trees, shoot cans for target practice, and hunt rabbits for their evening meals. The friendly locals often bring them onions, potatoes, and tomatoes from their gardens. Francisco witnesses a parade with an honored guest—Tito, the communist leader of Yugoslavia, is there to celebrate the troops of the International Brigades. The date is July 14, 1938. Commissar Tito drinks to their health.

The Battle of the Ebro

One morning the platoon is given new uniforms, an indication that they will soon be deployed. Then they are told to check their weapons and prepare their rucksacks with canned food, toiletries and other supplies. Now, Francisco is certain they will see action. The next day they are taken to a beachfront on the Ebro. The chief of staff, Major Malcolm Dunbar, briefs them on the plan of attack. The operation will take place south of Corbera and Gandesa, two towns in a mountainous area not far from the river. The attacking forces call themselves "The Army of the Ebro." It is now July 24, 1938, and this will be the last major battle of the civil war.

Francisco is assigned to lead his platoon across this river under the cover of night. At one in the morning they receive their orders by courier. As before, the Finn wades across and attaches a nylon line to a tree. Each member of the platoon, familiar with the routine, pulls himself to the far bank. Once on the beach, they disguise themselves in Nationalist uniforms. Behind them, other platoons begin to cross the river, some in rubber boats. Their orders are to advance toward Asco and Flix, while Francisco's platoon heads toward Corbera and Gandesa.

Francisco's volunteer soldiers proceed along the path guerilla style, spaced ten yards apart. They cross a narrow bridge and come upon a house whose windows are illuminated by kerosene lamps. Francisco dispatches four men to kick down the door; they return with seven Civil Guardsmen. When Francisco interrogates them, the guardsmen's answers are unhelpful. They are stabbed to death with daggers, their corpses thrown into a ditch on the roadside. The platoon now changes from Nationalist uniforms to those of the Civil Guardsmen. Francisco marvels how perfectly his uniform fits. They make their way back to the bridge and post two soldiers at the entrance, while two others wait nearby in pit-like holes.

When a military truck approaches, Francisco fires his gun in the air to signal it to stop. Finding his vehicle surrounded, the driver steps out of the cab and raises his hands. Francisco allows the civilians to escape into the forest. Nationalist soldiers are taken as prisoners, but the two Civil Guardsmen that climbed from the back are killed.

Nationalist soldiers soon come running toward the bridge in bunches. These soldiers want to surrender; full of panic, they shout and argue among themselves. Some speak bitterly of Franco as they plead for their lives. A few race beyond the bridge and vanish into the forested hills. Because there are so many, Francisco lets them scatter—all but the officers, the Civil Guardsmen, and the Moroccans, whom they shoot. In the end, twenty are killed on the spot.

Then another platoon of volunteer soldiers arrives, the one that had previously gone toward Asco and Flix. The two groups are glad to see each other and are relieved that neither has suffered major casualties. They rest, smoke cigarettes, and wait. When Francisco is ordered to organize an ambush at Corbera, the two platoons climb into the recently captured truck. They dismount a mile from town, then advance guerilla style along the fringes of the highway. Because they are dressed as Civil Guardsmen, they are able to kill any unsuspecting enemy troops who approach them without caution. A squadron of Polish cavalry arrives to bolster the offensive.

At dawn a motorcycle courier arrives with instructions to attack. The platoons advance, cautiously hugging the storefronts, buildings, and stone walls as they make their way to the center of town. They are soon fired upon. Two of Francisco's men are killed by a machine gun set up in a bakery. Francisco signals several of his men to follow him to the back entrance. A few minutes later one of his men sends a grenade through the front window. When they enter after the explosion, they discover a woman seated in a chair, dead from shrapnel, her tommy gun still in her arms. In the cellar, three German pilots cower behind sacks of flour. During the ensuing struggle, one pilot wounds the Belgian soldier in his right thigh, prompting Francisco to kill all three pilots with his revolver. Francisco helps the Belgian up the stairs, sits him down along a kitchen wall, then goes outside, where bullets are chipping the masonry off the buildings that line the street. In the distance, he hears the sound of mortar shells exploding and the cries of the wounded.

Francisco and another volunteer squeeze into a nearby doorway littered with broken glass. Nothing happens for a while. Then four Legionnaires sprint toward them, firing blindly. When they're twenty feet away, Francisco steps from the shadows of the doorway and shoots them dead. The platoon next regroups near a cemetery, where Francisco assesses his strength: three of his men have been killed, one is wounded, and another is missing. Eleven volunteers remain. Meanwhile, the Polish cavalry is engaged in another part of the town.

They are permitted an hour of rest and are dozing under a tree when a courier rolls up on his motorcycle. Francisco learns that enemy soldiers have hidden themselves in the cemetery, which explains for him the echoes from the tombs. He is told to clear them out. Francisco calls for his men to check their weapons, shares one last cigarette with another volunteer, then leads his men into action.

They gather outside the cemetery gate then creep along the stone wall. At two in the afternoon, Francisco observes enemy soldiers crawling over a far wall. Although his platoon is weakened, he decides to attack. With the Czech behind a machine gun, the platoon advances. Once inside the cemetery walls, they dodge between headstones and hurl grenades into the tombs. When enemy soldiers emerge, bloody from shrapnel, they are shot or bayoneted to death.

The two sides exchange fire for several hours until the arrival of a hundred Republican soldiers, singing "The Internationale." The enemy is wiped out, mostly with grenades. Only five men in Francisco's platoon remain in fighting condition. He tends to the wounded before he makes his report at a post established on the main road near the bakery. A major gives Francisco ten more men on the spot: two Danes, a Finn, and seven Polish cavalrymen who have lost their horses in battle.

The platoon receives orders to head to Gandesa. They proceed cautiously and halt often to catch their breath. A young Republican soldier, wandering lost, is welcomed to the ranks with the gifts of a rifle, two grenades, and a hundred bullets. Immediately, he is an indispensable addition. Under an apple tree, Francisco is bending down to gather some fallen fruit when a sniper's bullet passes through his cap. This newest member of the platoon notices the flash from the sniper's rifle. Without waiting for orders, he moves stealthily from tree to tree, then pitches a grenade through the window of a small cabin. When the volunteers enter the cabin, they find a wounded Civil Guardsman, a pistol in his hand. They kick the pistol away and let him bleed. The cabin also contains two machine guns with ammunition, a crate of grenades, a shelf of canned food, and some cigars and cigarettes. They gather this booty and roll a grenade into the cabin as they sprint away.

In late afternoon they find a farmhouse with the door and windows open, the hearth ablaze with a cheerful fire, and platters of food on the table. But there is no one present in the house. Francisco is bewildered. He checks the barn and finds mules, horses, donkeys, cows, goats and rabbits—but no inhabitants of the farm. The exhausted men carry this unexpected feast to the barn. There they eat, settle in and sleep, two sentinels posted outside. The next morning a lookout spies a column of Carlists soldiers. Francisco calls for two machine guns to be set up on a hill above the farm. Realizing the platoon is outnumbered, he considers a retreat until one of his soldiers informs him that three companies of the Lister Corps are less than a mile away. These companies will add to their strength—and just in time.

The enemy column approaches with their rifles slung over their shoulders, the scouts inattentive. In the sky directly above them, enemy reconnaissance planes loop daredevil fashion, then skim the farm without firing or dropping bombs—why the inaction, Francisco is unsure. Although still outnumbered, Francisco launches an attack as the Carlists are crossing a slippery shelf of rock not more than a few yards away. He stands and sprays bullets from his tommy gun, while others add to the attack with rifles, machine guns and grenades. The enemy falls in numbers; some retreat while others roll down the hill, wounded.

Through smoke and confusion, Francisco observes four small enemy Italian tanks crawling toward them, with fifty or more Carlist soldiers emerging from the forest beyond the farm. The battle is in full force by the time the troops of the Lister Corps show up. Quickly, these new arrivals fix their machine guns on tripods. The Carlists advance and attack in a column, making no attempt to hide.

Francisco orders mortar cannons into action. The barrage sends the Carlists flying in gruesome pieces. Some enemy soldiers retreat to the edge of the forest or take cover behind farm implements. There's a pause in the battle before the enemy begins to deploy its own artillery. After a bomb explodes near them, Francisco and two others jump into the crater, reasoning that two bombs are unlikely to fall in the same place. The crater is still hot from the blast, the air thick with dust and smoke. Francisco gazes skyward: he makes out an enemy plane and, seconds later, hears the rattle of its guns. Just a few yards away, a soldier from the Lister Corps is targeting the plane with a machine gun. The plane loops up and away only to return to strafe them again.

Francisco observes the arrival of seven enemy tanks. There are Legionnaires, Moroccans and Red Berets crouched behind the tanks, nearly invisible from the trail of exhaust. Francisco directs his men to hold their fire. When the enemy is within twenty yards, the platoon unleashes everything they have: mortars, machine guns, rifles, grenades. Three tanks are destroyed, while four others turn around, leaving the accompanying enemy soldiers exposed. They drop wounded or dead; those who attempt to crawl away are either shot or bayoneted.

After a second lull in the fighting, the enemy begins a rain of mortar shells. Minutes later another wave of Legionnaires and Moroccans charges their position. The attack continues for almost an hour. Francisco's platoon and the Lister Corp troops are nearly overwhelmed when a battalion of Republican reinforcements appears and joins the battle. The tide turns in their favor.

Although the battle is not yet over, Francisco's platoon is relieved of duty. Ten of their men are dead, and the remaining seven are given three days to recoup in an orchard of fig trees. The survivors eat, wash their uniforms, tend to superficial wounds, and sleep. In the distance, the battle continues night and day, though with less intensity eventually, settling into an exchange of sniper fire.

On a rest day, while he is picking tomatoes in a farmhouse garden, Francisco is fired upon by a machine gun. The platoon scrambles to action: three men position themselves behind the house, while two others sidle along the wall. After they pitch some grenades inside, the wounded come running out: four Legionnaires, a Civil Guardsman, and two Red Berets. All are brought down within yards of the house. When a Polish volunteer reaches to retrieve a weapon from one of the enemy soldiers, however, he finds that the wounded man is only playing dead. The Pole is killed, but another volunteer finishes off the enemy soldier. The platoon returns to camp without their comrade.

On another morning enemy planes appear from the east and fly in formation over the orchard. The Czech scrambles up a tree and sits perched among the branches with his machine gun and three drums of ammunition. Francisco knows full well that there's no talking him down. So he orders his men to dig defensive holes near the trees and move their supplies behind boulders. From his hiding place, he counts eleven planes—the older Italian Breda. One plane soon begins to strafe a wide path through the orchard. From high in the tree, the Czech fires upon the planes as they strafe and drop bombs and grenades. When the attack is over, he has downed two planes. Only his tree survives; the others are splintered and smoking from the explosions. The Czech rappels from his perch, unhurt save for a few lumps on his head from ricocheting rocks and limbs.

That afternoon a liaison officer shows up with nine replacements, all well-armed and with supplies on their backs. These soldiers are the remnants of another platoon within the Garibaldi Battalion and include five Italians and four Frenchmen. The men of the platoon—Cuban, Mexican, Czech, Dutch, English and Irish—share their rations with the newcomers and quickly become friends. Their orders are to return to the Sierra de Pandols and retake the area where they had previously fought. On the march they pick up a young Catalan soldier—lost, he has been struggling with fear and hunger. The platoon now numbers a full sixteen. They continue to make progress, passing a slow-moving battalion headed for the front. In the distance, they can hear the sounds of artillery and planes. They hole up at a cave along with other soldiers who are preparing for the front. Each man is given a bowl of hot broth and a loaf of bread. Deep inside the cave, the wounded have been laid out on stretchers or placed on beds made of leafy branches.

The platoon arrives at Sierra de Pandols the next day. Corpses lie along the roads and in ditches; some have been hurled into trees from mortar explosions. The enemy has taken up positions in the mountain cliffs. Francisco's men press ahead, ascending partway up a nearly vertical cliff. From there, Francisco spots two Republican companies preparing to attack the enemy.

Hours pass as the platoon waits for instructions. Francisco calls for one of his men to get water from a spring not fifty yards away. They have a willing volunteer, an Irishman who fills four canteens before he is shot dead by a sniper. Feeling a responsibility to fetch the canteens, Francisco manages to reach the spring unobserved. He grabs the canteens and scampers back to his men, moving wildly from rock to rock and tree to tree. Bullets fly over his shoulder and head, but he is not hit.

At nightfall a company of Republican soldiers is ordered to take the hill. Under cover of darkness, tanks fire upon enemy positions. In response, the enemy soldiers toss grenades that skip down the rocks and explode among the advancing soldiers. Although Francisco's platoon was instructed to wait, he itches to join the battle.

An observer reports that there is a route up the cliff. Francisco and another volunteer climb up to reconnoiter. Francisco makes out an enemy machine gun, a system of trenches, and a line of soldiers, mostly Moroccans. He considers assembling his platoon for an attack, but a platoon leader requires permission for such an act. Francisco sends the soldier back to headquarters, at the base of the mountain, to inquire. A half-hour later, a major, a captain, and two lieutenants climb up to make their own assessment of the situation. The officers decide on a frontal attack as well as attacks from the flanks. The major instructs Francisco and his platoon not to start up the cliff until the bombardment begins. The officers climb back down while Francisco remains on the side of the cliff with three Andalusians, his platoon positioned behind him and ready to charge. The night deepens and grows cold. The Andalusians are prepared to throw themselves at the unsuspecting enemy—the first trench is not more than thirty yards away—but Francisco tells them that he has his orders and that they should wait.

When the Republican tanks and cannons begin the bombardment, Francisco and some veteran members of his platoon begin to crawl toward the trench and its momentarily quiet machine guns. They pause inside a fold of terrain to catch their breath and steel themselves. Ten yards away, they can hear the voices of the Moroccans. Five minutes pass, then ten, then twenty, before Francisco hurls the first grenade, killing four enemy soldiers at a machine gun. The skirmish begins. Through the smoke and dust, the Czech runs forward and jumps into the trench. He proceeds slowly along, firing his weapon as the Moroccans crumble. Some drop their weapons and attempt a wild escape. The Dutchman follows, mowing them down with his tommy gun as they begin to scramble up the hill behind the trench.

Francisco orders a green flare, a signal to the companies below that they can now move upward with less fear of gunfire and grenades. While inspecting the area, two platoon members are killed and another is badly wounded by enemy soldiers playing dead. Francisco's men are furious. Despite their cries for mercy, these enemy soldiers are shot or bayoneted. Francisco orders one of the Andalusians to descend the cliff and request replacements—and in a hurry. Nine of his men are killed or missing. The youthful Catalan soldier is at his side, nervously firing at any unfamiliar figure.

Some time passes. Two of the major's companies climb the summit in search of enemy holdouts. Finding none, they descend with Francisco's depleted platoon into a sort of valley, with Sierra de Caballs on their right. There they come upon some Italian cannons, seventeen trucks loaded with shells, and thirty-two Italian soldiers, who surrender without a fight.

The remnants of Francisco's platoon scale the back side of the Sierra de Caballs. The enemy has scattered, leaving their equipment and weapons behind. Here Francisco joins up with the 1st Company of El Campesino, the legendary guerrilla fighter. He and Francisco decide to conduct an assault on the Carlists at La Vuida, a mountain village. It is now daylight. They have been on the battlefield for nearly sixteen hours.

They take La Vuida after a brief firefight. When the battle is over, Francisco counts his men: he still has the Cuban, the Mexican, the Czech, the Dutchman, the Englishman, and the Finn, who is wounded from a bullet in the shoulder. He also has some of the newer recruits: two Frenchman, an Italian, and the youthful Catalan. That means he has lost six comrades somewhere on the windblown terrain.

Back at camp the wounded Finn is taken away on a stretcher and Francisco reports to the general staff. The platoon is granted one day of rest—and one day only. The following morning, they are to march back in the direction from which they had come, an area still active with snipers. They return to the plain at the foot of the Sierra de Pandols and walk along a gorge scattered with corpses. When the enemy suddenly attacks with mortars, the platoon holes up in a shallow cave, as other soldiers pour in. One shell hits the cave entrance. The Italian, a Frenchman, and the young Catalan are killed. Four others are wounded, including

Francisco whose leg is injured from shrapnel. The cave echoes with the howls of the injured.

Two stretcher-bearers from the XV Brigade, with help from Francisco's men, ferry Francisco and the Englishman down the gorge to a clearing near a road. Just as they arrive, two enemy planes appear from beyond the mountain and strafe them. On the planes' second pass, a tossed grenade kills the Cuban, Francisco's favorite comrade. The remaining soldiers lift the wounded into an ambulance then climb in for the ride to a makeshift hospital.

As the ambulance bumps down a road pocked with the craters of mortar shells, the two planes reappear. Again the planes attack with blazing guns and tossed grenades. The ambulance stops under some trees. The Dutchman jumps out in an attempt to take a defensive position. Sitting on the back bumper of the ambulance, the Czech opens fire with his machine gun. One plane's engine coughs black smoke and sputters. But the Czech's machine gun is now empty and he has no more ammunition. When the remaining plane launches its final attack, the Czech lays his body over Francisco. The wounded Englishman and the Finn are shot to pieces. The Frenchman is also killed. The Czech pulls himself off Francisco, unscathed.

The Dutchman runs up to the ambulance, believing all his comrades are dead. The truck's sides are riddled with bullet holes, the windshield is completely shattered, and the lifeless driver is slumped over the steering wheel. But Francisco, the Mexican, and the Czech are alive. He tells them the plane that strafed them has landed in the field. They go and retrieve the pilot—a German—who talks in German to the Czech, then soon bleeds to death.

They drive in the direction of the River Ebro. There they roll their dead comrades into a large hole where there are already other corpses. It is a sorrowful moment. Still, they go on. The Czech, the Dutchman and the Mexican board a truck, while Francisco is put onto a train to Sangre Hospital in Barcelona. He can hardly walk and has lost a lot of blood.

Francisco recovers among other wounded soldiers from the XV International Brigade. During one visit, the Czech opens up about his past and the roots of his devotion to the Republican cause. His wife had died while giving birth to a boy. The baby also died. To Francisco, the Czech's story is more painful than the war.

Francisco also receives a visit from Commissar Tito. The Czech, the Mexican and the Dutchman are all present when Francisco is honored with a Bronze Medal of the Spanish Republic and a Medal of Merit of the Ebro, and is made staff lieutenant. The others receive similar medals and promotions as well.

Commissar Tito toasts their bravery. Then they and everyone else in that wing of the hospital enjoy a large meal with wine and hard spirits.

The Hospital, the Last Battle

Francisco convalesces at Las Planas, a mountain resort turned hospital near Barcelona, among other soldiers from the International Brigades. He rooms with a Mexican, a Pole, and a German, all with severe wounds that won't allow them out of bed. The German has had a leg amputated, while the Mexican has severely broken legs and arms. The Pole is in the worst condition: a grenade went off in his hands. Doctors have reconstructed them, but they are roped above his head in grotesque display. The healing will take a month.

Some surgeons have proposed amputating Francisco's leg, but an English doctor argues against the operation. Instead, he cleans the wound with a long rod then pours a clear liquid into it—Francisco grits his teeth during the procedure. Within six weeks he is able to walk and even begins to romance a Catalan woman from Barcelona. Her name is Maria Lacanca, and she is an anarchist and true militant. She is so dedicated to the cause that she even killed her husband, a fascist sympathizer.

Although Francisco still hobbles, he is assigned duty as Officer of the Guard. Wearing the new uniform presented to him during his promotion, he polices the former hotel and its grounds. In the surrounding forest, he comes upon some vagabonds and learns of an exodus from Barcelona: citizens who fear Franco's forces will invade the city. These escapees live in camps and are often hungry. Francisco distributes surplus food from the hospital's kitchen. As word of his efforts spread, the area where the hungry congregate is named the "Forest of Peace." Francisco is referred to as "The Frenchman who is Chief of the Forest of Peace."

Francisco has tables and benches built; soon a soup kitchen is up and running. He sees hundreds fed daily, and becomes enthralled by a twenty-year-old Gypsy woman named Rosita, whose father is wheelchair-bound. At times the family has been so desperate that they survived on oranges washed ashore from cargo ships. Francisco spoils them with hot food and wine, and arranges a room for them on the ground floor of the hospital.

In spite of his recovery, his thigh still troubles him. He is sent to Mataró, a coastal town, where he receives daily electrical massages. When he returns to Las Planas three weeks later, he finds the hospital shut down and now functioning as a command center for staff, officers and visiting dignitaries. Only with much effort does he reunite with Rosita, and they spend a week together in Barcelona.

In mid-September 1938, Francisco is summoned by the general staff, who explain that the Nationalist Army had retaken territory up and down the River Ebro. He is authorized to form a new platoon. At the Karl Marx Barracks, he rounds up the remaining soldiers: the Mexican, the Czech, the Dutchman, and the long-convalescing Belgian. To these he adds eleven veterans from the International Brigades. He is granted two trucks: one is loaded with supplies and food, the other with military gear, including three machine guns and crates of grenades.

They caravan to Falset, a village near the Sierra de Caballs. With a bridge down, the river crossing is impossible. Francisco's platoon and a company of thirty soldiers under his command wait for the bridge to be repaired. At dawn they cross the Ebro and head toward the town of Asco. They progress two miles, rest, and continue again—a slow pace, Francisco is convinced, makes for a better soldier. Plus, his long recovery from his wound has left him unused to trekking with weapons and supplies.

Around two in the afternoon, enemy planes strafe and bomb their position. The Mexican has an arm torn off and a Frenchman and an Italian are killed. The company of thirty soldiers also suffers: three dead, nine wounded. A half-hour later two ambulances arrive to carry the casualties away. Francisco receives a slight head wound from flying debris. Still, they set off toward a heavily wooded summit, but when he hears a distant human cry Francisco instructs his men to take cover—a sixth sense warns him that something unusual is about to happen. In reconnaissance, he continues climbing with three other soldiers, but they find nothing. He sends the Dutchman down the hill to order his remaining soldiers to advance.

Not long after the Dutchman has left, Francisco is bewildered by one, then two, then ten Republican soldiers running past him in panic. Francisco yells for one of the fleeing soldiers to stop. The man explains that hundreds of Moroccans, Legionnaires, and Civil Guardsmen are climbing the summit as well—the two sides will meet and the engagement will be bloody. The soldier runs off, one of many apparent deserters. He has given up so wholeheartedly that he doesn't even carry a weapon.

Francisco's men congregate near the summit, and he explains the situation to them, without mentioning the deserters. He argues that they should continue uphill before the enemy can reach the top; that way they'll have a better position for shooting and for hurling grenades. He directs the company liaison to lead his soldiers to the left, then up the hill. His own platoon will head straight up. The two groups separate.

Francisco leads his men up terraced fields that peasant farmers have built to cultivate crops. Near the top, Francisco confronts another panicky group of Republican soldiers yelling, "Here they come!" They too appear ready to retreat, though they haven't yet thrown their weapons aside. Francisco encourages them to find cover.

There is no time for fear. Francisco orders two machine guns to be set up and has his men form a defensive line behind a stone wall. A mortar shell explodes near them, then two more, within yards of them. Francisco calls for his men to abandon their positions and attack—to retreat, he believes, would mean certain death. Through the smoke of the explosions, his men advance over the mud-sloppy earth. Twenty feet from the summit, Francisco makes out the company of soldiers he had sent to the left. He is relieved to see that they hadn't run off.

The platoon quickly forms a new line of defense behind rocks and trees. The Moroccans charge in bunches and are easy targets. Francisco signals his men to fire when they are twenty yards away. Within minutes, forty, fifty, sixty of the enemy are dead. Francisco's men hurl dozens of grenades that send the Moroccans running downhill. The Legionnaires begin to flee too. Francisco's men follow the enemy's retreat. At the bottom of the hill, they liberate about a hundred Republican soldiers who had been rounded up by Civil Guardsmen. Now they have an additional company of men armed with the rifles and grenades left behind by the enemy. They continue their pursuit for nearly two more miles and come upon a squad of Nationalist soldiers on mules. They take them without firing a shot and show mercy by not killing them.

At this pause in the action, Francisco assesses his platoon: the Belgian has been killed along with six of the newer recruits, and one has been wounded. Of the platoon's original soldiers, only the Czech and the Dutchman remain.

The platoon, the major informs Francisco, will soon face the Moroccans, who have dug trenches along a hill. He promises supplies and well-equipped reinforcements. Meanwhile, Francisco, the Czech, and the Dutchman are given biscuits, wine, water, and cigarettes. Exhausted, they rest against some trees, fall asleep, and wake to the roar of three tanks headed toward the frontline. A few minutes later a column of prisoners marches past them, heads down—they will soon be trucked to the other side of the river.

Francisco is approached by a liaison on a motorcycle, who hands him a new set of orders: they are to go down the road and wait by a demolished house. The three men follow the directive and, to their happy surprise, they discover a supply truck with crates of food, wine and tobacco. Francisco, the Czech, and the Dutchman rest for two days, occasionally taking cover when an enemy plane strafes the woods. Incendiary bombs suspended by tiny parachutes fall now and then, but no casualties occur.

On the third day a small group of reinforcements arrives, and which includes one officer and seven men from the XV International Brigade, plus thirty-three Catalan peasants, none of whom is seemingly familiar with any kind of weaponry. Francisco views the Catalan replacements as reluctant soldiers. After marching for a day, he runs across a major from the general staff and explains his orders and his concerns. The major suggests that, after arriving at his destination, Francisco find a company willing to take charge of the Catalans.

They spend the night in caves and set out at four in the morning, crossing the plain in darkness. At daybreak the mountains are quiet, lacking even the familiar crack of rifle shots. Francisco finds a pair of Nationalist Army pants and puts them on, then slides a dagger up his sleeve. He directs the platoon to advance, the soldiers spaced six yards apart, with the peasants on the right and the Republican regulars in the rear. He advises the Catalan leader to take cover in some brush and wait for his signal to proceed, then sprints ahead alone, moving from boulder to boulder. He stops on a slope and surveys the mountains through binoculars. Seeing no movement and hearing nothing suspicious, he hurries back downhill and signals for the Catalans to join him. He makes the agreed-upon birdcall several times, but there is no response. He suspects the peasants have deserted.

Francisco jumps into a muddy trench and keeps moving. Before long, he spots hundreds of Carlists in the near distance, the flag of the Spanish monarchy waving in the air. They are headed toward his position.

In a hurry to return to his platoon, Francisco leaps out of the trench. Immediately, he confronts a soldier wearing a red beret, the symbol of the Carlists, and gripping a tommy gun. Francisco throws his dagger, deeply striking the enemy soldier in the chest. As the man falls, he sprays bullets wildly, but none strike Francisco, who dashes down the trail. He stops when he hears a machine gun firing from behind a large rock. He circles around the boulder, then approaches at a sprint. Because Francisco is dressed partially in a Nationalist uniform, the gunner is unconcerned. Francisco drops down next to him. When the gunner asks for a new drum of ammunition, Francisco plunges a knife into the back of his neck. He takes the machine gun and continues downhill, where he discovers the Czech running toward him, empty handed—he had tossed his own machine gun aside after running out of bullets. The Czech fixes his new weapon on a tripod and positions himself behind a rock. He informs Francisco that many in the platoon are either dead or have been taken prisoner. In the distance, they can hear the rattle of machine guns and the reports of rifles.

Francisco leaves the Czech. Farther down the hill, he spots a cave with an antitank cannon guarded by two Moroccans. He catches them by surprise and shoots them dead with his revolver. Out of ammunition, he tosses the gun away. He exits the cave in search of a better hiding place and comes face to face with three enemy officers. Francisco stutters when asked the name of his company. When the officers raise their own revolvers, he has no choice but to surrender. Francisco is prodded along a path and handed over to a guardsman, who ties his hands behind his back and thrusts him among the other prisoners, but not before slapping him hard. The prisoners are herded to a campsite where a Moroccan paces about, muttering and kicking at the dusty ground. Suddenly, in a burst of anger, the Moroccan grabs one of the prisoners and cuts his head off with a curved knife. The blood shoots like a fountain from the fallen body. Furious at this brutal act, a Carlist officer slaps the Moroccan, who wipes his mouth and laughs as he walks away.

Francisco is led to an area near a ring of large boulders. There he discovers the new members of his platoon, hands tied behind their backs, being guarded by the Catalan peasants earlier under his command but now armed with tommy guns. The traitors smile evilly and taunt their captives. A few minutes later, they line up most of the prisoners at the mouth of a large pit and fire their weapons. Those who don't fall directly into the mass grave are rolled into it. A guardsman tosses in the head of the soldier who had been decapitated minutes earlier.

Francisco and a few others are spared. They are marched to a convoy of trucks a mile away, then loaded aboard. The convoy is heading toward Gandesa when Republican planes begin to strafe it. The trucks stop under some trees. Francisco and another prisoner consider an escape, but a Civil Guardsman has his rifle trained on them. Then the Nationalist planes—some German, some Italian—come into view. For the next hour, Francisco witnesses an aerial battle. Twenty-five Republican planes are destroyed. If the pilots do not die on impact, Francisco is certain that they will be shot or bayoneted as they climb from their cockpits. Those who parachute from their damaged planes will be killed when they try to run.

The prisoners arrive at Gandesa and are jailed in an olive-oil factory, with guards posted inside and out.

Captivity, November 1938-July 1940

Francisco's stay at the makeshift prison is brief. Along with forty other prisoners, he is transported by train to Zaragoza then marched to a set of wooden barracks in an undisclosed location. In the morning they and other prisoners are escorted by bayonet to a courtyard. A colonel of the Civil Guard, a small man with a big mustache, angrily reports the number of Nationalist soldiers killed the previous day. He pounds his baton on the lectern and raises a fist at the prisoners. He then walks up and down the lines of prisoners, tapping on a man's shoulder to indicate his choice. After a shove from a soldier, each selection exits the ranks. From the corner of his eye, Francisco watches the colonel consider him for a second before turning to the soldier next to him.

"Now justice will be done," the colonel yells.

The seventy chosen prisoners are lined up against a wall and shot. Francisco doesn't look away from his fallen comrades. The surviving prisoners are scolded, randomly whipped, and forced back to their barracks. That evening a priest gathers information from them—date and place of birth, family members, education, occupations, reasons for joining the Republican Army, etc. Francisco conceals his rank and position. To admit that he is a platoon leader in the International Brigades means immediate execution. Instead, he confesses an uncertainty as to why he joined the Republican side. He plays the young simpleton—he is then twenty-two—by shaking his bowed head at his foolish ways.

On the morning of the third day, a guard enters the cell and shakes the prisoner sleeping next to Francisco. The confused and groggy prisoner is led away, a guard on each side. Twenty minutes later: a volley of bullets.

The next day the prisoners are again assembled in the courtyard. They are given loaves of bread and cans of sardines, then loaded into boxcars packed so tightly that there is no room to sit. Their new prison is a ruined castle near Bilbao, which is cold, windy, and full of shadows. In the morning, they haul large rocks from the sea. In the afternoon, they throw them back into the sea. This is their punishment. If a prisoner complains or falls from exhaustion, he is shot. They must sing "Cara al Sol," the unofficial anthem of the Fascists, and salute the guards Hitler-style when they pass.

A few days later they are back on a train and headed to Logroño. They are taken to an old convent, where they are plied with hot meals, coffee and cigarettes. Francisco is confused by this hospitality until he figures out the intention: butter them up so that they might squeal. The kindness is over by the second night, however, when a gypsy steals a gun from a guard, shoots him and two others before being wounded in the belly. Rather than surrender, the gypsy jumps to his death from a balcony. The officers order the remaining prisoners whipped. Two are plucked from their ranks and executed at dawn. After this, the punishment is random. They are beaten or worse. At one midday roll call, eighteen are shot as the other prisoners watch.

One morning a month later, Francisco is among a group ordered out of the ranks, assembled into columns, and led away. Though he expects the worst, they are directed to an unfamiliar part of the prison where they are given new clothes, a metal dish, a spoon, and a fork. They sit down at long wooden tables to a banquet of roasted chicken, rice, potatoes and bread. They are then taken to a train station and shipped to a barracks that was once a hanger for a dirigible. Six companies are formed—a hundred in each—all wearing white armbands.

For the next two weeks the prisoners drill in groups of thirty, hour upon hour, offering Hitler salutes to officers as they pass for inspection. By then Francisco has become good friends with José Cortal, a Valencian who speaks French. They are among the prisoners trucked off to help unload cement, lumber, and other materials for bridge repairs. One day they embark on a freight train and end up in a forest. The next morning they begin to break rocks, hauled from a dry riverbed, to be used as gravel for road construction.

The prisoners put in ten days at this task. One man, subject to many beatings because of his simple nature, asks a guard for permission to relieve himself. Squatting by the river, he suddenly butts the guard with his head. He gleefully bayonets the guard a dozen times then escapes by floating downriver. As punishment, ten prisoners from his section are shot.

The prisoners are trucked to the village of La Olmeda de Jadraque, where they widen roads with gravel. Francisco works side by side with his friend José. After twenty days they are shipped to the village of Horna. There Francisco becomes a baker's helper. Acting on the sly, he brings loaves back to the barracks, where they are secretly devoured by José and others. He becomes a favorite of the baker's wife, who plies him with tobacco and glasses of wine or port. They often sing in the kitchen and share stories.

Because he speaks French, Francisco next becomes an assistant to a Parisian doctor. The doctor is there to help the wounded and injured no matter their political affiliation; he takes no side in the war. Francisco's circumstances change dramatically. He is fitted for a uniform and given a white apron and a medical kit. He lives in a big house, has a bed in the pharmacy, and studies medical books in his spare hours. He makes rounds with the doctor and is even allowed to accompany him on patient visits outside the camp. Recalling his mother's home remedies, he nurses the injured with massages and hot and cold compresses—human touch, he realizes, is a medicine in itself.

Francisco is given a commission as health officer and wears a white armband with a red cross. He now serves both prisoners and enemy soldiers—injuries and aliments know no politics. When the doctor is assigned to another unit, Francisco is put in charge of the infirmary. Although his medical knowledge is limited, he takes care of sprains, back problems, broken arms, and smashed fingers—typical injuries of men who pulverize rocks and pave roads. For fevers, he dispenses aspirin, cold compresses and blankets.

The prisoners are dispatched to Baseilla, a town of four thousand, to repair a bridge damaged during an explosion. When that assignment is finished, they are sent to Cataluña. On each jaunt Francisco acts as a homeopathic doctor. His white medical armband and his commission as health officer allow him greater freedom, along with creature comforts such as a bed, double rations, and wine. Francisco is called El Médico Francés, "the French Medic." The nuns and priests consider him a miracle worker and try to fatten him up with hearty meals. There is even a feud over his services between a colonel and the commandant who intends to move Francisco's battalion to another camp. When Francisco is finally shipped off, he is laden with gifts and showered with kisses at the train station. The colonel embraces him and refers to him as his son.

In Guadalajara the prisoners work as ironmongers as they sort destroyed cars, trucks, tanks, old farm equipment, motorcycles, and all sorts of scrap metal. Using a combination of wit and commonsense, Francisco again plies his medical skills. His life is doubly good now: his friend José Cortal is with him.

Francisco is trusted. The frustrated commandant pleads for Francisco to straighten out the workers, as their output is lagging. In a week's time, he organizes the men into six companies. This improves camaraderie and results in fewer injuries. With a canteen set up, the workers are better fed and more productive. Still, Francisco feels uneasy: he knows that the scrap metal is bound for Italy, a Fascist country, where it will be melted down for new weaponry.

With the work running smoothly, he reassumes his role as medic. The sick and injured ask for him by his nickname, El Médico Francés. He becomes a favorite among the nuns in this new place as well, even briefly taking the mother superior as a lover (twice a week he visits her privately). After three months in Guadalajara, however, the battalion is trucked to Alcalá de Henares, fifteen miles northwest of Madrid, the scene of some of the final battles between the Republicans and the Nationalists in late 1938. The prisoners are tasked with cleaning up the barracks damaged by grenades and bombs, and hauling away the rubble caused by mortar strikes on the local cathedral.

When Francisco is interrogated by a priest, he reveals nothing of his connection to the International Brigades or his involvement in the war. He pleads indifference to politics and political organizations and refers to his youth—what young man of twenty-two knows what life means? The next day twenty-eight prisoners who had been more forthright in their interviews are led away. They are shot at a camp outside of Guadalajara, their bodies rolled into a mass grave. Francisco receives a sentence of thirty years in prison.

Not long after this incident, the battalion of prisoners returns to Guadalajara. Francisco broods over his sentence—thirty years of crushing rock and sorting metal! He and others once again become militant. Using bottles from the pharmacy, a little wire, and coils of copper, a radio is constructed. Now they can hear news about Nazi Germany, and about Mussolini and his army's atrocities in Ethiopia. The state of the world angers and emboldens Francisco. He begins to study hand-drawn maps in preparation for an escape. He queries fellow prisoners about railroad lines, highways, lakes and rivers, and paths through the mountains. He asks his most trustworthy friends for their home addresses, friends who themselves secretly harbor plans for escape. Because a failed escape would mean execution on the spot, Francisco prepares carefully.

One day he goes to the arms depot and tells the sentry on duty that he must report on the available armaments. The sentry waves him inside. Once inside the armory, Francisco grabs an automatic pistol, bullets, two grenades, and a dagger, weapons which he hides in his jacket. He next reports to the officer in charge that the hospital needs him for an urgent case. When his pass is immediately approved, Francisco strolls out of the prison.

This is the summer of 1940, a year and half after the defeat of the Republican Army. Francisco has been in captivity for nearly two years. At heart, however, he is still a volunteer soldier. He has not forgotten his dead comrades and he does not know what has become of his friend, the Czech. But he remembers how the Czech draped his body over him when the plane strafed the ambulance. What better comrade could there be?

Fueled by bread and wine—gifts of the bartender's wife in Guadalajara—he embarks along a trail into the forest. He wonders what day it is, or even what month. Just hurry up and move, he tells himself, and heads toward Aragón by following a river. When his rations are gone, he lives off wild apples. On the fourth day he meets some woodcutters, who share their meal and inform him that the area is controlled by Falangist soldiers. Soon he is in familiar country and able to use the mountains of La Olmeda and Horna as landmarks. The village of Siquenza is not far—or so he is convinced.

About ten days after his escape, he encounters two Civil Guardsmen in the road; neither of them shows alarm as Francisco approaches walking along the road. He shoots them dead and confiscates their pesetas, a lighter, and brand-new Mausers. He drags their bodies into the brush.

A day later he locates the house he had been searching for. When he was a prisoner working as a medic in the area, he often obtained bread and meat from the two women who lived there, in exchange for cans of milk pilfered from military supplies. The husband of one of the women had been killed by a Falangist. Francisco waits until dark to knock on the door. He is greeted with hugs, invited inside, and offered food, wine, and a warm bed—a luxury after his many days of sleeping on the ground.

The next morning he rises from bed to find his clothes washed and ironed. The women tell him that two other men who fought for the Republican cause are hiding in a nearby granary. The three come together in the evening and begin to plan a journey to France. Vicente fought for the Durruti Column outside Madrid; Luis was a political commissar in the Lister Corps. Francisco recounts his time in the International Brigades and his many battles. Vicente and Luis feel confident; Francisco feels purposeful. For him, the death of an enemy of the Republican cause is justifiable, and an escape to France would represent a worthy achievement.

On the evening before their departure, they share a meal with the two women. Francisco gives a pistol to one of them—you never know, he cautions her. She presents him with a switchblade knife that he had been admiring. He puts on his "costume," a Francoist uniform; his two comrades dress in peasant garb. With their rucksacks heavy with provisions, they kiss the women goodbye. It is three in the morning.

Guerrilla Warfare, July 1940 to February 1941

After a year spent hidden in the granary, Vicente and Luis become panic-stricken whenever they encounter a passerby on the road. Francisco understands their jitteriness. During their frequent rest breaks, he teaches them how to handle and throw a dagger. He also provides instruction in loading and carrying their weapons and introduces hand and birdcall signals. Luis appears the more soldierly of the two, often caressing the wooden armature of his outdated rifle.

By day two they are near the village of Horna, where the remnants of Francisco's platoon were rounded up and held as prisoners. He instructs Vicente and Luis to remain at the edge of the village, as he wishes to pay a private visit to the baker's wife. She is both happy and worried by his sudden appearance. Her husband is still in prison and life is hard. The local priest insists on tithes from the villagers—each week they must give him something or the Civil Guardsmen will come calling. Twenty-five villagers are in prison because of this priest, and many luckless farmers are dwelling in caves or tents in the countryside.

The baker's wife offers Francisco's two loaves of fresh bread. Pressing some pesetas into her palm, he asks her to buy as much tobacco as she's allowed (tobacco is rationed and difficult to come by). She returns after a few minutes and contributes her husband's tobacco, stale but still worth smoking. She adds some peaches as a farewell gift.

Francisco exits the bakery in broad daylight, greeting a few of the villagers he recognizes from his time there as a prisoner. He proceeds down the road to the rectory where the priest lives. With cap in hand, he raps on the door. He begs the priest to hear his confession. The priest appears doubtful but allows him into the foyer. Within seconds Francisco plunges his dagger between the priest's shoulder blades, then rakes it across his throat. The priest falls to the carpet, a pool of blood spreading widely. Francisco rifles through the drawers in the priest's office and brings out a thick envelope: 11,200 pesetas. From the kitchen, he takes a loaf of bread and a roasted chicken. Then he makes a silent promise: the pesetas are from the poor and will go back to the poor.

Francisco rejoins Vicente and Luis; he doesn't tell them about the priest's death. They start across fields, come to a range of mountains, then skirt the edge of the forest. Soon they come upon a small train depot defended by three Civil Guardsmen; the tracks lead to Zaragoza. Francisco decides to attack after the next train from Zaragoza arrives, lets its passengers off, and leaves for Soria. Two more guardsmen get off the train and join the others. Toward late afternoon Francisco tells his comrades that it's time to attack and that they should checks their weapons

Francisco runs from behind a pile of railroad ties toward the guard post—Vicente and Luis follow on his heels. Through the open window, Francisco can hear voices and the click of dominos. He tosses a grenade through the window. All but one of the guardsmen are killed. He shoots the uninjured one with a Mauser. Vicente gathers the men's rifles and revolvers and searches the bodies: 3,100 pesetas. They smash their own outdated rifles they had been carrying against a post.

Two depot employees shake with fear on the platform, their hands raised skyward. Francisco tells them that he doesn't kill unarmed civilians. Then he, Vicente, and Luis hurry away in the direction of Zaragoza. Once in the forest, they reverse course, as the civilians might report on the direction of their escape. They sleep in the forest and set off the next day through high mountains ten miles north of Ariza.

On the third day they encounter three woodcutters, who warn them of bandits, as well as the military police and Civil Guardsmen that patrol bridges, crossroads, and the entrances to villages. Francisco gives each a thousand pesetas, bread and cheese, and some tobacco. The woodcutters are grateful; they have been hungry for a long time.

The fugitives camp near a stream and shoot two hares, which they skin and roast over a small fire. After this meal, Francisco builds a larger fire then instructs Luis and Vicente to move to higher ground—he has an idea. Before too long, two soldiers in ragged Republican uniforms appear. The soldiers search the campsite and kick at the embers of the dying fire. Then three other soldiers join them. Their faces show disappointment at finding nothing to eat. They are walking away, rifles on their shoulders, when Francisco steps out from hiding, points a revolver, and orders, "Manos arriba!" The soldiers lift their rifles from their shoulders, surprised but ready to fight. Francisco yells that, like them, he is a Republican, that his comrades are Republican. With a bloodbath avoided, the men embrace. Although the war has been lost, the soldiers say that they would prefer to die in the forest than surrender.

Francisco gives each man a revolver. Their names are Pepe, Luis, Manuel, and Antonio; the fifth goes by Sanchez. These new recruits lead Francisco and his comrades to a cave in the mountains. That evening they share a single loaf of hard bread and the leftovers of a roasted wild boar, and discuss their escape to France. It is decided that Francisco, though younger than most of the men, will act as leader. Cans of food and boxes of biscuits are divided among them. Their arsenal includes three tommy guns, eight automatics with clips, nine grenades, and two hundred bullets.

The next morning they set off in the direction of Zaragoza. They move guerrilla-style, practicing maneuvers as they go along. Three days into the journey, their provisions are exhausted. Francisco risks knocking on a farmhouse door. The farmer is alarmed by his disheveled appearance and becomes truly afraid when Vicente enters roughly. In the kitchen, a boy of twelve begins to cry. Francisco assures the farmer and his family that they mean no harm. They are just hungry, he explains. Right away the farmer stuffs a cloth sack with five loaves of bread, a ham, some morcilla sausages, and salted pork. He tops off Francisco's canteen with wine then goes to his garden for vegetables. By this time the boy is holding Francisco's hand; they have become friends. When Francisco tries to pay the farmer a thousand pesetas, the farmer waves him off. But Francisco insists. This is the way of the guerilla, he argues.

The men follow a ridge toward Zaragoza. After two more days, they encounter a column of soldiers patrolling the mountains. The enemy passes not thirty yards from where they are hiding in the undergrowth. Francisco decides that there are too many soldiers to risk an attack. That evening they wade a small river and walk along train tracks that climb a mountain range.

Again, their provisions have run out. They encounter a woman herding a single goat, her daughter at her side. Francisco asks about her husband. She sizes up this band of weary looking men. He's in France, she openly tells him, a former Republican soldier who managed to escape after the war. She begs them to join her and leads them to her farmhouse.

While the other men relax in the barn, Enrique, Luis, and Francisco accompany her to the village to buy provisions, where the shopkeeper offers them supper. The talk is boisterous, though Francisco doesn't reveal much about their journey. When Francisco pays generously for the provisions, the proprietor throws in chocolate bars and cans of tuna. Upon their return to the farmhouse, they are surprised by the appearance of women and children milling about, all of them curious about this band of former Republican soldiers. The men are greeted like heroes, and a barber gives each a haircut and shave. Francisco is unconcerned about the apparently widespread knowledge of their presence. After all, the locals side with them.

The next morning their hostess brings them bread and bowls of milk, then walks them to the edge of the village. Her little girl kisses each man good-bye. Two days later they reach a large village where two Civil Guardsmen are stationed at a bridge. Francisco and Enrique stroll toward the bridge. Francisco is dressed in a Nationalist uniform, Enrique in peasant garb. They shoot the unsuspecting guardsmen and confiscate 410 pesetas, two handguns with ammunition, two light rifles, four grenades, and a single can of food.

They cross the bridge into the mountains. The next day Civil Guardsmen, military police, and a few locals pursue them. The guerillas circle part of the way down the slope, then sneak cautiously from tree to tree until they find themselves *behind* the pursuers. Francisco cries his *grito*, "Hai!" With tommy guns, they open fire on the enemy—six or more are killed in an instant. After this success, the men push on. An hour later they encounter three Civil Guardsmen on the road. Francisco approaches at a natural pace, then hurls a grenade at them. His comrades finish them off.

They next confront a Civil Guardsman on horseback. They shoot him, but a shot from the guardsman's revolver strikes Sanchez in the shoulder. They hurry away, Sanchez with his fingers in the wound to stanch the bleeding. They climb slope after rolling slope, distancing themselves from the enemy. They fill their canteens at a spring then come upon a cave to hide in for the evening. Francisco probes Sanchez's wound and, using a pair of scissors, manages to pull out the bullet.

They build a fire, eat, smoke, and drink what little wine they have. They rest in the cave for another day before setting off at dawn for another part of the forest. After three hours, they come upon a cultivated hillside of grapes and fruit trees. They enjoy these fruits and pocket as much as they can carry.

Then an ambush occurs while they are descending into a small valley. Caught in the open, the men race for cover behind boulders and trees. Francisco manages to protect himself behind a small rock wall. He assesses the situation: the enemy is firing automatic pistols, not rifles or tommy guns. Two of his men are missing. They are low on ammunition and the machine gun has only two extra drums. Francisco orders a frontal attack with grenades. They run toward the enemy's position, toss the grenades, and exchange fire with what turns out to be a group of mostly military police. After the ten-minute battle, twenty-seven enemy soldiers are killed and three are captured. Among Francisco's band, Valero, Manuel, and Luis are killed. In addition to his injured shoulder, Sanchez suffers from head and belly wounds. Francisco ends his agony with a single bullet.

The remaining four men collect the enemy's ammunition and pull a large wad of cash from one of the dead policemen's pockets. They now have a total of 37,850 pesetas. But their most useful find is a pair of binoculars. Saddened by the deaths of their comrades, they push ahead along the ridge and soon come to a wheat field. Francisco consoles his comrades and speaks of their bravery.

Peering through binoculars, Francisco is able to make out Alcuneza, a large village with a railroad station on the Madrid-Zaragoza line. He decides to advance through territory once held by the Republican Army during the war. But first he interrogates the prisoners, who tell him that they have been patrolling the forest in search of soldier named *El Mexicano*. Then he executes all three, even though one is only an adolescent, which causes him remorse.

The four men take a direct route to Alcuneza, come down from the hills, and wander into the village. Francisco is still dressed in his Nationalist uniform, while the other three are in peasant garb. To the Civil Guardsmen in the plaza, they appear as harmless locals. They pass through the center of the village without suspicion and within the hour are once again in open country. They cross an orchard and take refuge in an abandoned cabin. Before they have time to search the cabin for food, two Civil Guardsmen gallop up on horseback. Francisco signals his men to exit by the back door.

One of the guardsmen breaks open the front door with a rifle butt. He rushes inside, searches the premises, then comes out minutes later, seemingly disappointed. Francisco's men sneak around to the front and open fire. They drag the bodies inside the cabin and remove the guardsmen's clothes. Antonio and Enrique put on the uniforms, while Vicente remains in peasant dress. Not wishing to be weighed down, they abandon most of their extra weapons. They return to Alcuneza, where they board a bus for Valencia.

Francisco assumes the role of a Francoist soldier as he walks down the aisle of the bus, randomly ordering passengers to present their identification papers. Sometimes he lifts his eyebrows in feigned concern before he sighs and hands the papers back without a word. He smirks at Vicente, who holds back a smile at Francisco's posturing. He takes a seat next to a woman who senses that he and his men are anything but Francoists. After all, two of them have ragged beards and they all smell like a barn. Their uniforms are dirty, their boots non-standard issue. Francisco appreciates her confidence and good humor.

They have been traveling for two hours when the bus is flagged down by military officers whose car has broken down. A colonel and a Carlist commandant board the bus and sit near the front. Francisco neither meets their eyes nor speaks to them. The bus continues onward for several miles before Francisco signals with a whistle for Enrique and Antonio to force the driver to stop. The bus squeaks to a halt at a bend in the highway, the door is opened, and colonel and the commandant are prodded off.

While the bus rolls away, Francisco and his men shove the colonel and commandant into a field. They protest against this outrageous action until Francisco asks, "How many men have you condemned to death in your region?" The Francoists grasp the situation. The commandant cries, "*El Mexicano!*" Francisco shoots him, while Vicente shoots the colonel. Francisco and his band flee up the mountain. From the summit Francisco watches the village of Mondova through binoculars. Two police vans are setting out for their daily patrols. A single truck is also leaving—with soldiers or supplies he's not sure.

Francisco and his men backtrack down the mountain, cross the road, and trudge up a series of slopes until they reach a marble quarry. They rest in a shallow cave, not daring to start a fire. Although they have little to eat or drink, they take the opportunity to sleep a few hours. That night they break camp under a full moon. They are soon climbing a large mountain covered with esparto grass, which they pull up in clumps and chew. At dawn they encounter workers collecting esparto. The workers complain that their lives are miserable, for the landowner pays them little. Francisco listens with sympathy, then asks about the village and the possibility of buying provisions. One of the workers points out a canteen just beyond the trees. Francisco gives him money to purchase bread, sausages, and tobacco, and he and another worker depart.

Thirty minutes pass, then an hour. Suspicious, Francisco, Vicente and Enrique head out to investigate. They approach the canteen, where they hear bantering talk and laughter inside. One of the workers who had been asked to get provisions staggers out, undoing the buttons of his pants. He's relieving himself against a tree when he notices Vicente and Enrique. He doesn't run more than a few steps before Francisco, positioned behind a stack of crates, stabs him just above his heart. He lets out a cry and falls onto a pile of firewood.

Hearing the commotion, two Civil Guardsmen appear from the canteen and are shot before they can raise their rifles. Francisco and his men burst into the canteen to discover eleven frightened men at a table of half-eaten food, the air cloudy from cigarette smoke. Francisco lines them up against the wall. Vicente goes into the kitchen, where he recognizes the other worker who had been sent to get provisions. He shoots him dead as the culprit stutters an excuse, then tells the women huddled there not to fear. He searches the body for their pesetas and recovers that amount along with a larger wad. Outside, Francisco goes through the pockets of the dead guardsmen then returns to the canteen. Francisco tells everyone to eat and drink as he and Vicente throw a total of 645 pesetas onto the table.

As they leave, the workers inside the canteen raise clenched fists into the air and yell, "*Buena suerte, El Mexicano! Viva la República!*"

The men climb back up the mountain and trek toward the town of Pinoso. The first person they encounter is an aunt of one of Francisco's soldiers. She lives in a cave on the side of a mountain very near the town. Her life has been tragic: her husband sided with the Fascists and was shot by the Republicans. The army then forced her son to throw all the religious relics from the local church into a bonfire before imprisoning him. After the Republicans were driven out, the son was set free. Rejoicing, he introduced himself to the new mayor. When the mayor learned that the young man—despite siding with the Francoists—was responsible for the burning of the relics, he had him and thirty other sympathizers executed for the sacrilege.

On the third day in the cave, the wife of a friend that they had hoped to meet comes to see Francisco. She is employed as a housecleaner for a commandant, a spiteful man. Her husband, a former Republican soldier, has been exiled in France. With sorrow, she speaks of her poverty and how the town's diet is mostly carrots, although the surrounding fields are abundant with apples, sweet potatoes and ripening corn. Those fields, however, are patrolled by the Civil Guard. She takes the men's uniforms and returns them, washed and ironed, the next day.

Francisco and his men remain in the cave for eleven days. But before they resume their journey, Francisco ventures into Pinoso. He goes to the café, where the mayor is carousing with friends and lackeys. Francisco orders a bottle of wine and listens to the talk for an hour before he pays and leaves. Then he lies in wait in the dark until the tipsy mayor begins to amble home. Francisco calls out his name. The mayor turns and, in a nasty tone, asks what he wants.

"Justice," Francisco answers before he plunges a dagger into the mayor's heart.

Francisco returns to the cave with plans to leave in the morning, but he learns from a peasant that Civil Guardsmen are patrolling the routes out of the town. They stay four more days. On the fifth day, they depart before sunrise and escape over a mountain. They find themselves on an isolated road, with Enrique and Antonio dressed as Civil Guardsmen, Francisco in a Francoist uniform, and Vicente in peasant attire and playing the part of a prisoner. When a truck appears, Francisco waves for it to pull over. Seeing the rifles and tommy guns pointed him, the truck driver has no choice but to pick them up. Although their eventual destination is Valencia, they demand that the driver stop at Sueca, a small town where Francisco hopes his friend José Cortal—who had intentions of escaping from prison—might be living. The truck stops on the outskirts of town. They allow the truck driver to go his way, then walk toward the plaza. Francisco learns from a local that his friend did escape and that he and his family live in a granary outside of the town.

Upon their reunion, Francisco and José hug and dance in a

circle. Francisco observes that José and his family are very poor. His three children are shoeless, his wife thin and wearing a ragged coat for warmth. Over a small fire, a soup of carrots and lentils simmers in a pot. There are no sausages hanging from the rafters, no butter or cheese in the pantry. Still, Francisco and his men are honored with a bottle of wine. Francisco explains that he has come to take José to France. José is overjoyed at first, but quickly becomes reluctant as he can't bear the thought of leaving his family.

Francisco understands his friend's concerns and decides to help him. On their second night in Sueca, he and his men rustle vegetables from a nearby garden. On another night, he gathers sheaves of rice from the fields, a risky endeavor—eight peasants have recently been shot dead for such foraging.

Realizing that he must do more, Francisco borrows a mule from a neighboring farm. He and his men select a house whose residents are rumored to be well-off. They watch from a distance. When nothing appears out of the ordinary, they knock on the door. Without waiting for a response, Francisco enters, his Mauser drawn, while the family is seated for their evening meal. Although two of the intruders are disguised as Civil Guardsmen, the family understands that they are not what they seem. One of men picks up a butcher knife, but Vicente shoots him in the arm. The family cowers against the wall and the children begin to cry. Francisco apologizes for their roughness, attends to the wounded man, and assures the master of the house that they mean no harm. We just need provisions, he declares. The master begins to fill sacks with turkeys, chickens, rabbits, a goose, rice, lard, bread, and other foodstuffs. Francisco gives him six thousand pesetas, again apologizes to the wounded man, and with his men drinks to the family's health.

The men load the mule and disappear into the night. They return the mule to the farmer and give him five hundred pesetas for the use of the animal. When they arrive at the granary, José and his family look in disbelief at the food, which will last several weeks if not a month.

Francisco and his band remain hidden at the granary for a few more days. They depart under the cover of darkness after Francisco hugs his dear friend good-bye—they will not see each other again. At dawn they reach the sea near Valencia. They purchase grilled sardines and mackerel from a fisherman and devour this fresh catch on the beach. By nine o'clock that morning, they are strolling in the town center dressed as Francoists and Civil Guardsmen and carrying their rifles on their shoulders.

Francisco leads them to the apartment of a former prisoner known as El Grande, a retired boxer, who now works for the railroad. El Grande's parents greet them warmly. Francisco sees that the family is poor and offers the father tobacco and cigars for use in bartering—the black market is one way the citizens of Valencia get by. When El Grande returns from work, there is much hugging. To celebrate, Francisco gives the father several thousand pesetas to purchase food from a nearby market: melons, oranges, chickpeas, ham, and bread.

While his men bathe and relax, Francisco goes with El Grande to a club frequented by boxers, local politicians, and Falangist officers. They flirt with some women for a few minutes, but keep to themselves and mostly talk about the tragedy of the war as they recall the names of comrades killed in battle. Tipsy, they return home and sleep. At daybreak El Grande leads them to the edge of town, past cane fields, to a small river that flows toward the city of Castellón de la Plana. Francisco gives his friend a thousand pesetas before they part for good.

They follow railroad tracks, an unerring guide for their journey. By nightfall they can make out the lights of Castellón de la Plana. They come upon a brightly lit house with music coming from inside, then give full attention to a car as it drives up the long drive and stops—three Civil Guardsmen get out and cheerfully enter the building.

Francisco decides to attack. Antonio and Enrique, dressed in their guardsmen's uniforms, approach the front steps, where the sentries are smoking cigarettes. Francisco and Vicente creep unseen toward the house and up the porch. They hear loud talk, laughter and music. Francisco peers through a window: enemy soldiers are playing cards and drinking. While Antonio and Enrique shoot the sentries, Francisco hurls a grenade inside. Before the smoke clears, Vicente shoulders the front door open, enters, and tosses a grenade into the main salon then another after the smoke begins to clear.

Antonio leaps over the dead and starts gathering the money from the cash register. Vicente opens the back door, where a frightened commandant stands with his hands in the air. He shoots him dead. Francisco fills a sack with tobacco, rum, and cognac, then gives a cursory look around the room. He is surprised to see a captain of the guardsmen staggering wounded toward him—and shoots him dead.

As the men are about to leave, Enrique calls out that a car is approaching. They hurry into the yard and take position behind a laundry shed. Two non-commissioned officers and a civilian emerge from the car, unaware of the bloodbath that has just occurred. They take a few steps, then are riddled with bullets. Francisco is going through one of their wallets when a blast from a tommy gun hits Enrique in the arm.

Because the shots came from the second floor, Francisco opts not to retaliate. He and his men scamper away while music from inside the house still plays on the phonograph. They hurry through a connecting series of vegetable gardens until they find a shed near the edge of the city, then settle in for the night. Francisco cleans Enrique's wound and the men divide their booty: each man gets nearly 90,000 pesetas, along with a ration of food, tobacco, and cigars. They've also captured two automatic pistols, five clips, and a Mauser. Francisco reckons the number of casualties: three Civil Guardsmen, one captain of the guardsmen, seven Falangist officers, one commandant, four air force lieutenants, three captains, one civilian, and two non-commissioned officers from the car. He regrets not killing the soldier who injured Enrique—a grenade would have done the job.

At daybreak Francisco goes out to the edge of the vegetable garden. Through binoculars, he observes two ambulances and a van of military police. At seven that morning, a farmworker appears. Francisco assures the startled worker that he intends him no harm, gives him three cigarettes, and invites him to a meal of bread and sausage. The starving farmworker accepts the invitation—the man's daily ration is a piece of bread, a pot of rice, and green beans. They talk a while before the farmworker excuses himself to begin weeding his garden patch. Vicente follows him to make sure he doesn't sneak off to report on them. At one in the afternoon, the farmworker returns to eat with Francisco and his men. Then they all nap on the ground.

Late in the afternoon, they stuff vegetables from the garden into rucksacks and once again share a meal with the farmworker. Francisco gives him five hundred pesetas, two packets of cigarettes, five cigars, and a sausage—their bond is complete. In return, the farmworker presents the men with a rare gift: a bottle of wine.

At nightfall they set out on the road.

The Band of El Mexicano

Francisco's men have trekked four days and nights when a large factory with tall smokestacks comes into view. Nearby there is a barracks-like prison enclosed by rolls of barbed wire. Francisco studies the prison and chooses to wait. They spend the night in a cave huddled together against the cold. The next morning Francisco observes activity at the prison: a column of prisoners exits, guarded by four Nationalist soldiers and a single Civil Guardsman. The prisoners trudge toward the factory. Francisco and Vicente follow them at a distance, make note of a bombed-out house, then wait in the brush. At six in the evening, the prisoners, weary from work, return.

Francisco and his men spend another night in the cave. At daybreak they go out and wait for the prisoners to reappear. At about 7:00 a.m., they see them plodding along in a column of thirty, with two Civil Guardsmen in front, four Nationalist soldiers in back.

Francisco needs more soldiers for his escape to France and is determined to pull volunteers from the prison ranks. He outlines a strategy for attack. The men check their rifles and pistols and fill their jacket pockets with grenades.

Francisco and Enrique position themselves in the roadside brush, while Vicente and Antonio wait further down the road. When the column of prisoners passes, Francisco and Enrique mow down the two Civil Guardsmen in front, careful not to hit any of the prisoners. Antonio and Vicente yell for the soldiers at the end of the column to raise their hands. Without being asked a second time, they drop their rifles. The prisoners are confused by this sudden onslaught. Who are these attackers? Bandits?

The prisoners calm down after Francisco explains his intentions to cross into France and asks who will join them. Five men step forward immediately, followed by a second group of six. He gives them the weapons of the fallen guardsmen and the captured soldiers. Francisco hands out cigarettes and cigars to the remaining prisoners, instructing them to wait in the bombed-out house until the hour when they usually return to the prison.

Francisco and his men return to the cave with their new recruits and four captives. He ponders their next move, sleeps a few minutes from exhaustion, and wakes. He moves downhill to check the scene through binoculars and is upset that the prisoners have disobeyed his orders. Instead of staying in the house, they are milling about outside. When he observes the arrival of some military personnel, he retraces his steps to the cave. He orders the captured soldiers to remove their uniforms and promises not to kill them. One of them asks if he can join the guerillas. Francisco considers the man for a few seconds before nodding his head in agreement. After questioning the new volunteers, he discovers that most fought for the Republican cause, while two are political prisoners.

Francisco distributes additional weapons to his new recruits, who are astonished to hold something other than picks and shovels. He gives each man twenty bullets, and some receive grenades as well. He tells them that he has been schooled in guerrilla tactics and—if they adhere to his commands—they have a chance of survival. They trek for three miles before Francisco releases the three Nationalists, all very young men with fear in their eyes. He asks them not to return to camp until late afternoon—for the sake of their fellow deserting soldier. They promise to say that they got lost after their release, then shake Francisco's hand.

Two of the new recruits are familiar with the area. Following their advice, Francisco leads his band through brush and over slopes. Because the new recruits are poorly shod and weak from overwork and hunger, he calls for frequent rest breaks. The prisoners are scared; they imagine enemy soldiers lurking behind every boulder.

They stray from a wheat field into an apple orchard, where the recruits gather the late fruit that has fallen from the branches. They rip corn from an unattended patch to roast later over a fire. Now that they are farther from the prison, the men feel less jumpy. They wash in a ditch, enjoy their fruit, and take refuge inside a barn. At nightfall, the least exhausted among them stand watch over the others.

During the night Francisco considers the quality of his new platoon: Vicente, Enrique, Antonio, Mier, Mendoza, Planero, Luis, Manuel, José Sanchez, Luis, Pedro, Quadiola, the "black" Antonio, and Mechol, the deserter. There are now fifteen in all and mostly armed, though not the soldier who has deserted. A few are experienced fighters, with one having held the rank of lieutenant in the Republican Army. Others are unaccustomed to being in the open and flinch at every movement—even the wind through the trees frightens them.

At sunup Francisco divides the men into squads. He offers a machine gun to Mechol, who is grateful to be trusted. Francisco clambers up a hill and through binoculars catches sight of four Civil Guardsmen on horseback. Perfect for an ambush, he decides. He tells most of the men to remain in the barn and calls for four of his most experienced soldiers to follow him. Mechol, in a Francoist uniform, is told to proceed down the road, stoop at the first sighting of the enemy, and pretend to be tying his shoelaces.

The Civil Guardsmen come around the corner, looking left and right. When they catch sight of Mechol, they approach at a trot. They are no more than a few yards away when Francisco and the other men open fire—the bullets puncture their bodies and send them flying off the horses. The guardsmen are stripped of their uniforms and weapons, plus apples and sausages from their rucksacks, and a pair of binoculars.

Nearby, fieldworkers, frightened by the shots and the sudden galloping of a riderless horse, barricade themselves in a barn just beyond the road. Ten minutes pass before a brave, old woman comes out to investigate. Small as a child, she confronts Francisco. In a kind voice, he begs her not to fear them, assuring her that he and his soldiers are not thieving bandits. He asks for bread and water and presses a thousand pesetas into her hands. Two young men soon return with one sack full of bread and another filled with various provisions.

Francisco ties two of the horses to a tree and shoots a third injured during the exchange of gunfire. The fourth horse has run off. This worries Francisco because the horse is likely to return to the enemy camp. At the barn where his new recruits have been waiting, he distributes the captured weapons and gives the guardsmen's shoes to those whose feet will fit.

The men make their way down a road for two miles, then circle back—Francisco explains that it's often wise to feign escape then return to the site of the skirmish. In mid-afternoon two vans of Civil Guardsmen appear. Peasants emerge from the fields. Francisco can see by the peasants' gestures that they are revealing what had happened and who is responsible. They point to a nearby farmhouse half-hidden in the trees. The officers discuss the matter among themselves, then all but two of the guardsmen climb back into the vans and drive away. The remaining guardsmen barge into the farmhouse after a single loud knock on the door. After a while, the old woman and the two young men who delivered the provisions are pushed roughly outside. There is an exchange of words and pleas. Rifles are pointed at them.

Francisco and Vicente quickly climb down from their position. But by the time they get to the farmyard, the old woman has fallen to her knees with a guardsman's rifle pointed at her forehead. The guardsman kills her and is turning to the two young men when Francisco shoots him. Nevertheless, bullets from the guardsman's final shots strike and kill the young men. Vicente shoots the other guardsman and, rushing forward, Francisco plunges a knife into him—his anger is immense.

Other people rush outside from the house. After Francisco recounts what has happened, they carry away their dead without a word. Meanwhile, Francisco and Vicente remove the guardsmen's shoes and uniforms, and take their ammunition, plus 428 pesetas. Their rifles are smashed against a tree.

Now well-shod and dressed as Civil Guardsmen, Francisco's men parade openly, two abreast, with Vicente in the center as he plays the part of prisoner. Toward evening they come to a large plain that is mostly red earth and dry grass. Francisco considers crossing it, but worries that the moonlight will reveal their movements. Instead, they camp behind a shelter of rocks and don't risk building a fire. They break camp early in the morning and journey over the plain toward the forest. Soon they encounter a patrol of seven Civil Guardsmen on horseback. Minutes later, Francisco observes a second unit of guardsmen. The enemy, he sees, is intent on setting up two lines of fire.

It's time to move—and with urgency. In groups of two or three, the men advance from tree to tree, boulder to boulder, bush to bush. Suddenly, the Civil Guardsmen are in full gallop. Some are firing their revolvers while others blaze away with tommy guns. Antonio, known as the black Catalan, rises in panic and begins to run. He is cut down immediately.

With the enemy nearly upon them, Francisco's men begin to fire. The guardsmen fall, some dead and others injured. A few dismount and charge. In the end, twelve are killed and two escape on horseback. Three of Francisco's band are dead and one is gravely injured. Francisco puts a bullet in his head to end his suffering. They have lost Luis, Planero, and Quadiola. Manuel has an injured hand, which Francisco cleans and bandages.

After collecting the guardsmen's ammunition, grenades, and provisions, they proceed at a hurried pace through the forest. At nightfall they come upon a farm with three goats in the yard. Francisco and Vicente approach the house and peer in a window to look upon the family at dinner. Francisco knocks softly. An old man comes to the door and sizes them up, not in the least worried. Although the family appears to be poor, their dinner is abundant, with three lit candles in the center of the table. The old man invites them to join them for dinner. Francisco thanks him, then calls his comrades inside—all but two who must stand guard. They eat cabbage soup flavored with bacon and topped with fried eggs. The women of the house silently appraise the soldiers and refrain from conversation. After dinner, the old man—without being asked—fills a sack with bread, meat, and two gourds of wine. Francisco pays him a thousand pesetas and asks for peasant clothes, which he pays for as well.

After saying their good-byes the men march for three days along a mountain path. Their food is soon gone and they survive on acorns, apples, and tender grass. Although they are tempted to shoot the numerous rabbits that leap from the underbrush, they fear the echo of gunfire might alert the military police that patrol the area.

Three more days pass. In dire need of food, Francisco commits his men to an ambush near Zaragoza, once a Republican stronghold. They take positions on both sides of a quiet road. When a truck with a military insignia approaches, Francisco gives what has now become the battle cry of *El Mexicano:* "Hai!" They fire on the truck, killing the driver and his companion. The truck rolls into a ditch and settles there, nose down. In the back of the truck, they discover three crates of canned food and bottles of wine, along with boxes of canvas shoes with rope soles, the kind that Legionnaires wear. In the truck's cab, Vicente finds a metal box full of money.

Minutes later a small car appears on the road, which they stop. Two peasants get out, cautiously putting their hands in the air. One asks for an explanation, but his question is ignored. Vicente peeks into the car: live chickens and a basket of onions; he takes both. Francisco gives the peasants a thousand pesetas, more than enough for what he has taken, and lets them drive away. Then the men hustle further into the hills. Under a tree they roast the chickens and onions, and open cans of sardines and other food. With wine and cognac, everyone is cheerful. Francisco counts the money in the box: 33,440 pesetas. He distributes the canvas shoes to his men.

That evening, well rested and with bellies full, they set off again. The temperature is near freezing. Toward morning, on the outskirts of an unnamed village, they stumble on some woodcutters hunkered down before a roaring fire. Noticing that they look hungry, Francisco offers cognac and sandwiches piled with leftover chicken, plus some tobacco. Their new friends describe the nearby villages and how they will be bustling with Legionnaires and Civil Guardsmen, that the farmers are stingy. They offer their blankets to Francisco and his men, pointing out that they can get others back in their village. Touched, Francisco offers them two thousand pesetas.

Francisco and his men arrive at a narrow river and follow it to the edge of the first village. As the woodcutters foretold, it is swarming with enemy soldiers. They stay clear and proceed along the river, which has widened and will eventually feed into the Ebro. On each side are small gardens, where past-their-prime fruits and vegetables remain for the taking. They stumble upon an isolated barn and set up camp. The next day they reach Villanueva, where they encounter two peasant women on the road. The women are frightened at first, but quickly realize that Francisco and his men aren't bandits. They tell Francisco that they work on a nearby farm and speak of the owner's kindness. Francisco admits that they could use some supplies. Without another word, the women hurry to the house and return with eight loaves of bread, three large wedges of cheese, and sausages and ham. He gives the women three thousand pesetas.

They bid the women farewell and ask them to thank the farmer. They trek about a mile before they eat and rest. After they smoke some cigarettes, they follow a river and head up a mountain. Near the summit, Francisco uses his binoculars to scan the area below. He spies enemy soldiers seated around campfires, a convoy of trucks, and three tanks making their way down the road. Francisco feels that they must keep moving, so they cross a bridge, scale another mountain, and follow the river's course from a distance, walking along trenches dug during the war. They salvage some unexploded grenades and a rusty machine gun. Later, they will disassemble it and rub the parts with olive oil and butter, but for now, with rain coming down, they find shelter in a wooden hut.

The next morning they descend to a road, skirting a village and keeping to a forested area. In an alley of chestnut trees, they pause to rest and open the last cans of sardines. Francisco sends three men to check on an abandoned convent. They return and report that the convent is now occupied by enemy soldiers. Francisco goes to see for himself. Through binoculars, he observes soldiers milling around two trucks. Francisco signals his men to head back up the mountain.

They are walking on a path next to a larger road when the enemy trucks swing into view—one comes to a stop on the left, the other on the right. They're trying to encircle us, Francisco surmises. He decides to return to the convent where, he suspects, a few enemy officers and soldiers remain.

With the bulk of the Legionnaires in the mountain, the guerilla fighters surround the convent. Francisco and Vicente creep ahead, make their way to an enclosure near the convent wall, then forward, unseen. They pause there for a few minutes before Francisco goes one way along the convent wall while Vicente goes in the opposite direction. Two sentries are posted near the large wooden door, neither very alert. When a lieutenant comes out to talk to them, Francisco shouts "Hai!" and tosses a grenade. Seconds later, Vicente hurls two more grenades. Once inside the convent, Francisco and Vicente find the dead and gravely wounded lying on the floor.

Manuel, the Andalusian, rushes into the courtyard to finish off the wounded sentries, disobeying Francisco's orders to wait for a signal. He is killed right away by a burst of machine-gun fire. Francisco and Vicente look at each other—the floor above, their eyes say. They mount the stairs, their steps muffled by the rifle shots below. The machine gunner is surveying the yard, the long, smoking barrel of his gun resting on a windowsill. As he turns his head, Francisco kills him with a revolver. In an adjoining room, a mess hall, four Legionnaires raise their hands in surrender. Francisco shoots them all.

Francisco and Vicente go back downstairs to count the dead: three commandants, two captains, and two lieutenants. But the guerillas also suffer losses: Antonio and Mendoza, both good fighters, are surprised by five Legionnaires in the kitchen, though they manage to kill or wound their attackers as they fall. In the melee, two Alsatian wolfhounds tied to the kitchen table are also killed. Vicente finishes off the wounded still squirming on the floor.

The men undress the dead officers and put on their uniforms, including the capes, caps, and plumed helmets. They collect three tommy guns, drums of ammunition, and better-quality grenades. Francisco tells Mier to splash kerosene throughout the rooms—they will burn the convent. Meanwhile, Vicente and three others, dressed as enemy officers, make their way to a footpath, where a truck is being nervously guarded by two soldiers. When the unsuspecting soldiers ask about the gunfire at the convent, they are killed by a burst of fire from a tommy gun.

Luis drives the truck to the convent, where Francisco and the others are waiting. A fire now roars inside, the timbers crack, and smoke billows from the windows. They drive off in the direction of Zaragoza. The boxes in the back of the truck contain leather boots, a machine gun with three drums of ammunition, twenty-two grenades, and 4,800 pesetas. There are also ten loaves of bread, sausages wrapped in newspaper, oranges and apples, and canned beef and sardines.

Pedro, one of the newer men, is familiar with Zaragoza from his military service. Before entering the town, he advises that they ditch the truck. They will avoid the town and head to higher ground by following the electrical powerline that runs from Zaragoza to Barcelona. That night they take refuge in a hut. At dawn they continue their journey, moving in groups of four with Vicente as scout. From the top of a hill, Francisco observes a railroad station swarming with activity—not only enemy soldiers but also merchants and families. With so many locals milling about, Francisco believes that they will go unnoticed in their Legionnaire's garb. They descend to the highway and enter the town.

The men brave a stop at a tavern, where they enjoy ham and

sausage sandwiches along with wine. Without asking for the bill, Francisco pays the bartender 2,500 pesetas. The bartender is delighted. The men drink more wine, smoke cigarettes. They then disappear back into the hills in search of the powerline. Not an hour later they encounter four Civil Guardsmen on horseback, set up an ambush, kill them, and take their machine gun. The old machine gun that they reconditioned with olive oil and butter is discarded.

Now acting as scout, Pedro suggests that they climb yet another mountain. Although he sees that his men are exhausted, Francisco agrees. They descend, meander through a valley where a stream flows, and begin to climb again. There are few trees or shrubs on this mountain, the cliffs are slippery, and the wind is bitterly cold. Near the summit Pedro spots what appears to be a column of about twenty Legionnaires. After studying their uniforms through binoculars, however, he thinks that they might be German soldiers instead.

For Francisco, there's no choice: an ambush. Machine guns are set up on both sides of the trail. They wait behind some boulders. When the German soldiers are ten yards away, they mow them down. But Francisco and his men are taken by surprise. A smaller column of Legionnaires that had been marching behind the Germans rushes forward to attack. In an exchange that lasts ten minutes, they too are shot dead, but Francisco's ranks suffer as well: Luis, José Sanchez, and Pedro are killed. Now there are only five remaining: Vicente, Antonio, Mechol, Mier and Francisco. They strip their dead comrades of revolvers, bullets and provisions, leaving the bodies where they fell. At the summit, Francisco sees a wooded mountain that Pedro described earlier. Through binoculars, he makes out the powerline they will follow to Barcelona and eventually into France.

Across the Ebro

Descending into a valley, Francisco and his men encounter a boy tending goats. The boy doesn't seem alarmed—what war? his shining face seems to say. When Francisco asks about the land-owner, the boy describes a mean man who carries a rifle wherever he goes. Francisco gives the boy a hundred pesetas and pats his head. The men make their way to the edge of the farm and rest there for an hour as Francisco weighs the risks of an attack. He decides to send Vicente, disguised as a migrant worker, to recon-noiter. He and the others crouch behind an old tractor, within shooting distance, in case trouble erupts.

With a revolver hidden in his waistband, Vicente saunters up to the wrought-iron gate. He whistles and calls out several times for the landowner. Eventually, a man about fifty emerges with a hunting rifle. He wears an old sweater and new corduroys held up by suspenders. As he steps down from the porch, he asks the stranger what he wants. Vicente yells, "Work, sir." The landowner looks him over and demands his papers. Two more men, both bearing arms, appear from the house.

Francisco senses danger and rushes out from behind the trac-tor. The landowner looks up at the sound of boot heels hitting gravel, startled at the quickly approaching figure. Francisco shouts "Hai!" which sends Vicente falling protectively to the ground. Francisco drops the landowner with a burst from his tommy gun. Mier and Antonio bring down the two other men.

Quiet fills the air, the pristine silence that follows gunfire. Seven farm laborers, all unarmed, come forward from different directions. Some salute Francisco and his men with clenched fists, the Repub-lican gesture of solidarity. To them, Francisco and his men are sav-iors. Three women emerge from the house, return inside, then soon return one by one with bread, cheese, sausages, and wine from the kitchen—the stingy landowner can't stop them now. The killings and the rejoicing occur within the span of half an hour.

Francisco pulls 1,300 pesetas from the pockets of the land-owner's sweater, which he gives to the women, in addition to 4,000 pesetas from his wallet. They leave with rucksacks full. About a mile and a half down the road, they encounter two Civil Guards-men on horseback. They pick off one and wound the second, who rides away slumped in his saddle.

Back in the mountains, they march two days southeast toward Catalonia, where Francisco was taken prisoner in November 1938. Their provisions are nearly gone. Although Civil Guardsmen patrol the area, often harassing the locals, the men are desperate for food and willing to try anything. Francisco throws a grenade into the river and the river throws up fish, which they grill on a spit. To supplement the meal, they gather nearly rotted figs and olives that have dropped onto the leafy ground.

When they come upon a village, Vicente and Mechol, dressed in fine corduroy, are sent to buy provisions. They soon return with good news: the baker welcomes them. The men wash, have haircuts and shaves, eat and drink, and warm themselves before the oven. The baker loads their rucksacks with fresh bread, cured ham wrapped in newspaper, and replenishes their canteens with wine. Francisco gives the baker a thousand pesetas. Braced by this hospitality, they leave at dawn. A day later they meet a poor peasant family and stay with them for three nights. They help the family cut firewood and eat very little, as the family has next to nothing. With candles snuffed out early, there is nothing to do but sleep.

The men proceed into unfamiliar terrain: ravines and gorges and the distant sound of waterfalls. But as they approach Grandesa, Francisco remembers the battlefields. They stand before muddy trenches littered with rotting uniforms, rusty weapons and helmets, crates that once held mortar shells, unexploded grenades half-hidden in mud. Wooden crosses mark the dead of both Nationalists and Republicans.

They avoid Grandesa. Soon Francisco recognizes a mill where he was once held prisoner for two days without water or food.

He sends Vicente and Mechol ahead to questions some peasants. They learn that the mill owner is a stingy and mean-spirited Falangist leader, who resides in comfort at a nearby farm, with Civil Guardsmen patrolling his property. Francisco decides to pay him a visit. The farmhouse is a rich man's chateau surrounded by a park and well-tended vineyards, now leafless in late autumn. Two wolfhounds accompany the guardsmen on their patrol of the farm. Francisco devises a plan: that night they will throw rocks against the kennel. The dogs will howl and then one or more of the guardsmen will investigate the disturbance.

And so it goes. Two guardsmen come out, scolding the dogs to be quiet. Francisco brings them down with a burst of fire from his tommy gun. Vicente and Antonio, positioned near the front of the house, run to the window and pitch grenades inside. All is quiet until another guardsman begins firing his rifle blindly into the night. Minutes pass before the guardsman jumps from a side window and runs unknowingly toward Francisco, who kills him point blank. After the melee, silence. Francisco waits behind a tree for Mier and Antonio to come out of the house. For ten minutes he hears nothing except the occasional scraping of footsteps. He is worried but doesn't leave his post. Finally his comrades appear with sacks over their shoulders. Mier is pushing the Falangist leader with the barrel of his rifle. The man, who serves as the local judge, seems more angry than scared. They kill him at the edge of the farm then make their way into the hills. When they look back, orange flames brighten the night. Vicente has splashed gasoline in the kitchen before lighting a match and sprinting away.

Francisco takes inventory of the two sacks: bread, smoked ham, boxes of cigars, and 117,000 pesetas taken from a drawer inside the house. Another 4,200 pesetas are pulled from the dead Falangist's pockets.

That night they break into a hut among an olive grove and sleep with their revolvers in hand. The next morning they set off through the plains and roam through a series of connecting orchards, avoiding contact with farmworkers and shepherds. When badgered by the police, the peasants will even snitch on their neighbors. They trek three days. Each evening they choose an abandoned house or hut in which to sleep.

One morning Francisco spies twenty trucks of Civil Guardsmen. He next catches sight of six guardsmen on horseback surveying the countryside. His worry deepens when eleven more trucks rumble past, these carrying Red Berets. "The hills will be swarming," Francisco whispers to himself. He watches through binoculars as a patrol of Civil Guardsmen push two peasants down a path. Francisco realizes that they will be interrogated and, when they can provide no reports of guerrilla activity, shot. There is nothing he can do.

When it begins to rain, each man covers himself in a tarp. They mark time under a canopy of trees, but the rain doesn't let up, so they begin to march. They follow a muddy path that runs alongside orchards, purposefully avoiding the mountains where Red Berets and Civil Guardsmen will be on the prowl. A mile up the road, they catch sight of two trucks parked beside an old house and pause to watch them. The rain doesn't let up. An hour later the enemy soldiers hurry off the mountain, their uniforms caked with mud, and get into the trucks.

After the trucks depart, Francisco and his men investigate. Inside the house, they find one old man and two young men dead from bayonet wounds. In a hallway, an old woman is face down, dead. A low fire burns in the fireplace. Francisco sends one of the men into the cellar: he returns with two small casks of wine, moldy figs, cans of sardines, and loaves of bread wrapped in towels. While seated at the table, Francisco hears a creak in the kitchen. He stands up, revolver in hand, and tiptoes into the kitchen. When he lifts the lid of a wooden barrel, a boy of about twelve cries for mercy. Dry lentils fall from his head and shoulders as he stands up. Francisco caresses his head in an effort to calm him down.

With tears in his eyes, the boy recounts how soldiers barged into the house and demanded to inspect the family's papers. Perhaps upset at the tone of his grandfather's reply, they stabbed him and the boy's older brothers to death. As his grandmother tried to run, they stabbed her also—the bayonet wounds are in her back. When two neighbors came to see about the commotion, they too were bayoneted to death.

Francisco is unsure about what to do next, but when the boy begins to stuff a rucksack with supplies, he realizes he has no choice. The boy must join them; otherwise, he will be killed by the Civil Guardsmen when they return on patrol. The boy's name is Fernando and, as Francisco soon discovers, is a good scout. As they move through the hills, the boy points out which houses are abandoned and which are occupied by peasants. Soon they come into view of Corbera. From a summit, Francisco uses his binoculars to survey the terrain below. He doesn't spy any guardsmen, but senses that they are tracking them. They march a little longer, then rest in an abandoned house. There, Francisco teaches the boy how to load and unload an automatic pistol. The eager boy shows him how to use a slingshot. They have become friends.

The nights turn freezing cold. Sometimes they snack on nearly rotten vegetables picked from frost-tinged gardens. Once Francisco kills a snake, skins it, and roasts it over a fire—but only he and the boy are willing to try this unusual catch. On another night, a young family makes room for them in their farmhouse. Francisco bakes bread and cakes on a sheet of iron set over a roaring fire. He gives the family a thousand pesetas and two packets of cigarettes before the men move on. To stay any longer would put the family in jeopardy.

They slip away in the darkness, cross a railroad line, and find themselves nearing the Ebro. They advance cautiously to the slow-moving river, where four boats are moored on the bank. Francisco sends Fernando to ask an old man sitting on the bank if the boats are for hire. The boy does as he is as told and explains that he and his friends want to fish. The old man gets up from his stool and gestures for the boy to follow him. In a whisper, Francisco orders Vicente to accompany them—Vicente is on his feet in seconds and hollering for the boy and the old man to wait for him. The three make their way toward a shed. As they reach it, the old man trains a pistol on the boy and yells, "Reds!" Two Civil Guardsmen jump out from behind the shed and seize Vicente and Fernando.

Francisco witnesses their capture through binoculars. In desperation he sends Mier and Enrique across the train tracks with the intention of attacking the shed from the rear. When the two signal that they are in position, Francisco runs toward the shed, yelling "Hai!" He tosses a grenade in front of the open door, hoping to startle the guardsmen and allow Vicente to overpower his captors. Mier tosses a grenade onto the roof with the same idea.

After the explosions, Francisco rushes inside and finds the guardsmen wounded. He takes a dagger to them. The old man is on all fours behind the fireplace, and Francisco kills him with a single shot from his revolver. The boy has been torn to pieces by shrapnel, and Vicente suffers from bullet and shrapnel wounds. He explains what happened: Fernando, unable to control his anger, called the guardsmen criminals, crying that they had murdered his family. The guardsmen killed the boy—he was dead before the grenades exploded.

The men carry Vicente from the shed, then paddle across the river in a boat. They lift Vicente out, place him in a thicket with his tommy gun, embrace him goodbye, then race away. Vicente understands that this is only way to help his comrades.

On reaching higher ground, the men take cover behind rocks. Francisco looks through his binoculars: enemy soldiers are slowly approaching Vicente. When they are nearly upon him, Vicente's gun spits bullets. Five soldiers fall. Two get up and stagger toward Vicente, who shoots himself dead.

Heavy hearted, the band of men sprints away, crosses an orchard, and works their way up a hill. From there Francisco observes the enemy marching in a line down a path. The guerillas descend the hill and set up an ambush in an open space by hiding behind large boulders. Francisco instructs his men that when they hear the first burst from his tommy gun they should toss one grenade each at the enemy.

They wait half an hour. The enemy draws near, chattering among themselves. One soldier looks up and sees Francisco, who has risen from a crouching position with his tommy gun. Francisco fires on the line of soldiers. After the grenades are tossed and the air clears, the men count among the dead four Falangist citizens. Normally they would collect weapons and inspect rucksacks, but this time they don't dare: some of the fallen may be playing dead. The men return to the highway, then follow their ever-constant guide, the powerline. They walk all day and part of the night, exhausted, cold, and hungry. They spend the night in a grove of hazelnut trees that Francisco recognizes as the place where he took target practice. The village of Molerussa is not far away.

The resourceful Francisco snips three feet lengths of copper wiring and shapes them into snares, a technique he learned from the Finn, long dead. His comrades laugh at him, but by the day's end he has captured seventy-two rabbits. They feast on six of them, then smoke the remaining rabbits and wrap them in paper.

Francisco sends Mechol to Mollerussa to inquire about bartering the rabbits with the local restaurant. An hour later he reappears with two boys carrying sacks. They stuff the rabbits into the sacks and all of them—the four men, plus the two boys—visit the village. The restaurant owner greets them with cognac and bread. He plans to marinate the rabbits in jars. In friendship, Francisco offers him a box of cigars, and gives each boy five hundred pesetas. They dine with the family, then return to the cave on the edge of the village, with a gift of hams, sausages and bread from the restaurant owner.

The next day they decamp and again follow the powerline that rises and dips over the hills. They trek through an area planted with olives, grapes, carobs, and hazelnuts—all are out of season. They pass peasants going to and from the fields, but they are miserly in their greetings—Franco has made the country bitter. After two days they come upon the village of Torre de Fontaubella, where Francisco saw action during the war. He asks a passing farmworker, "Who's the mayor?" The worker, visibly unhappy at the question, snarls that it's the same mayor as before the war. *Traitor*, Francisco broods, remembering him as a stingy public servant. He had once gone to the mayor and asked for oil and domestic rabbits, but the mayor would neither sell nor give him any. Everything was for the Nationalist Army; better yet, everything was for *himself*.

That night they pay a visit to the mayor's house. Francisco knocks on the door and asks to purchase bread and wine, to which the mayor responds angrily that he has nothing! Francisco eases his way inside, the mayor backing up when a revolver is pointed at his face. His comrades slip in behind Francisco. Mechol and Antonio go from room to room then search the cellar, where they discover hundreds of bottles of wine, sacks of rice, beans, and lentils, and rows of canned beef and sardines. Smoked hams hang in the pantry, along with wreaths of dried vegetables. In an office drawer, Francisco finds 22,480 pesetas. *The miser has nothing*, he thinks bitterly.

Francisco does not believe in torture. Still, he cooks up a meal of sausages and eggs, slices cheese and bread, and pours his comrades glasses of wine. When he asks if he has an appetite, the mayor shakes his head no and looks down at the floor. There is no conversation, only noise from forks cutting into sausages and scraping the plates. After they finish eating, Francisco returns to the mayor's office for a piece of cardboard. He writes: "This is the way traitors to the Republic die." He signs it "*El Mexicano*." The mayor is executed in a hallway and the sign placed on his bleeding chest.

Loaded with provisions, the men leave the village and follow a crest of hills. On the third day after the mayor's execution, Francisco makes out some Civil Guardsmen trotting toward them on horseback. He and his men duck into an abandoned machine-gun post. Two guardsmen are so near that Francisco can hear their conversation, but he refrains from killing them as the rattle of guns would alert nearby patrols.

That night Francisco and his men hustle in the direction of a large mountain sparsely dotted with pine trees. From that height, they can view the sea and the moonlight on its surface. By following the coast, they will arrive in France.

Since his escape from prison, Francisco has carried a map drawn by a friend, a Catalan wood merchant. His friend offered his house—if Francisco should make it that far. But the house, they realize, is situated dangerously close to a Civil Guardsmen barracks. They go at night. With his men waiting in the shadows, Francisco knocks on the door. When the door opens, his friend beams with joy, and they hug. Francisco signals Mechol, Mier and Antonio with a birdcall whistle. That night they feast, bathe, and sleep on mattresses, a luxury. The next day his friend suggests possible routes and warns him that Barcelona is dangerous: guardsmen are posted not only at major highways and roads but also paths and foot bridges.

They depart that evening. Francisco and his comrades travel through gorges and ravines, with every intention of avoiding the roads. From the hills, they can glimpse the sea and are full of hope: France is just over there! They march for three days when they come upon what looks like an abandoned house. But they find a family dwelling there: two women, two children, and a man of about fifty. They use crates as furniture and clothes for blankets, and have nothing to offer their guests except wild apples and a pot of lentil soup. The men sleep on the floor. The next morning, Francisco gives the family a single loaf of bread, six sausages, tobacco and a thousand pesetas.

They push on toward Barcelona and risk strolling like tourists along the beach. Mechol undresses and, gripping a burlap sack, leaps into the cold surf. Minutes later he emerges with mussels and oysters. Francisco and the others collect crabs in the shallow cove. They build a fire and roast some of their catch, sprinkling it with vinegar. They boil the rest in an olive oil can and wrap the seafood in cloth. They climb a sandy cliff and don't get far before they encounter two Civil Guardsmen and a forest patrolman. In an ambush, they kill all three then collect their ammunition and a shotgun. The soldiers' rucksacks contain bread, a bar of chocolate, two partridges, and a rabbit. They hurry on, the sea always in view. At an abandoned bunker, they roast the rabbit and partridges, then nap, with one man keeping watch.

The next day they again descend to the beach, with Vicente, shotgun in his arms, presenting the image of a hunter. By dusk they are back on higher ground. Now they can see the lights of Barcelona and make out the blare of foghorns. They find a hut for the night.

The next morning they walk by farms on the outskirts of Barcelona. When they pass workers in the road, they tip their hats and wish them a good day. At noon they come to a large house with a courtyard and several barns. One barn is full of vegetables from the autumn harvest. When Francisco asks about the owner, an employee leads him to the house. The merchant is surprised— who is this unshaven stranger? A beggar?

Francisco explains how he needs to go to Mataró, a coastal town north of Barcelona. Would he be able to rent them a truck? The merchant responds that such a request is impossible; he has dozens of men working under him and must oversee his business. Francisco then discloses his military status and describes his travels from prison to this very house. The owner is unmoved. Francisco has no alternative than to be blunt: if the merchant refuses his request, he is a dead man. What will his family do with a dead man?

The merchant becomes pragmatic—business is business—and promises to drive them himself but in a car, not a truck. At road crossings, trucks are inspected by the Civil Guard. The mood becomes cordial after the merchant apologizes for his rough nature.

While Francisco goes to get his men, the merchant prepares fried eggs and ham and uncorks a bottle of good wine. After this breakfast, he loads the car with cases of dried fruit and packages of onions and garlic. Francisco pays him 15,000 pesetas.

Francisco asks that they make a stop before they leave Barcelona. He wants to say hello to Antonio Palmerón, a comrade from the war. The merchant agrees without complaint or worry. While the others wait in the street, Francisco hurries up a stairway carrying a single crate of dried figs, onions and garlic. His friend is overjoyed to see him, but their reunion is brief. Antonio understands the urgency—a car is waiting down below, his presence possibly dangerous. Francisco presses 15,000 pesetas into his palm.

When the car arrives at Mataró, Francisco asks the merchant to drive them to a forested area outside the factory town. The men disappear among the trees stripped of autumn leaves.

The Border

To escape Spain, the guerillas must cross a range of snow-laden peaks. They are still carrying a machine gun along with rucksacks stuffed with provisions. Occasionally, they pass woodcutters who silently touch their hats in greeting. Everything feels calm and the enemy seems remote. They follow the railroad tracks that lead toward Puigcerda, the last village before France, and arrive at a large chateau. Through binoculars, Francisco watches civilians come and go. Nevertheless, they detour around the chateau and trek for four days, resting in abandoned huts or behind the shelter of rocks to avoid the cold wind.

At Vich, a town renowned for sausage-making, Francisco

considers buying provisions. But he decides to avoid both the town and the highway with its occasional roar of military trucks. They tread along the smallish River Ter, which feeds into the larger Gerona, until they come to a plank that serves as a bridge for peasants. The weight of their weapons makes each footfall a springy step.

By this time they have little left to eat: only two cans of beef. Francisco decides to attack a Civil Guard post. They approach the small building at night. Francisco looks inside: the enemy soldiers are sitting down to supper, their last. When he tosses a grenade through a window, the explosion kills two outright. A third is badly wounded while another crouches behind a bed in a side room. After these are also killed, they gather bread, sausages, apples pocked from the explosion, and cans of food. Rifling through a drawer, Francisco pulls out a list of a hundred suspected Republican sympathizers in the area—this list he shreds with his hands. They grab boxes of bullets and a ten-liter demijohn of wine before they scramble back into the forest.

At dawn Francisco sights two truckloads of Civil Guardsmen traveling up the road, in search of them, he presumes. Francisco opts for digging holes in which to wait out the danger. They spend a day and a night in their burrows. On the morning of the second day, they emerge from hiding and set off again. At noon they come upon an enemy bunker. The soldiers are outside sunning themselves. Francisco and his comrades approach, one slow step at a time. When they're ten yards away, they open fire. Two are killed outright. One is wounded and nearly gets back to the bunker, but Francisco kills him with a grenade. Inside the bunker, they collect new automatic pistols along with plenty of bullets, and sticks of dynamite.

Francisco devises a bomb with a long fuse, which he places in the middle of the bunker. After he lights the fuse, they run hard. They are less than a hundred feet away when the bomb explodes. Rocks and debris fall about them, and a fire starts in the damp brush.

Hours later they reach a wooden bridge over a small stream. Through binoculars, Francisco watches the site and decides that it is unmanned, thus easy to destroy. They place four sticks of dynamite under a beam, attach two detonators and five yards of slow fuse. Francisco lights the fuse and hustles back to his comrades. They wait nearly half an hour before the bridge blows up.

The men proceed in short stages, alert and ready for danger. And danger suddenly arrives. Enemy soldiers pour from a farmhouse below. Though far away, the enemy aims and fires with machine guns. The bullets whizz past them, striking boulders and trees. Francisco and his men scamper away and climb the next slope. From the top, he can observe two separate groups of some thirty enemy soldiers each. One group is climbing directly toward them, the other is going around.

While the enemy struggles uphill, Francisco and his men stealthily descend, unnoticed. They cross the river at a shallow ford then start up another, less-wooded mountain. Their escape takes them into a cultivated area terraced with fruit trees stripped of leaves. The peasants timidly cast their eyes down when they pass.

Francisco is acquainted with the region and its village, Las Presas. He can see the church where, three years earlier, he had boarded a truck for Olot. It is there that the Ghirardelli Battalion, a commando unit, was formed. He scans the village through binoculars, observing citizens going about their daily business. When he trains his binoculars on a familiar farm, he notices a spiral of smoke from the chimney. The farm is a site of deep and tender memories. He and his comrades approach carefully; he tells his comrades to wait and walks toward the farmhouse, where a woman is pinning laundry onto a clothesline. He approaches her and, with his hat off, calls, "Amelia." It takes her a few seconds to recognize him. "Paco," she shouts in return. She runs to him and crumples in his arms, sobs, then leads him to the farmhouse. This is the daughter of the farmer who had welcomed him when he had first begun training as a soldier, who had fed him until he was nearly bursting, who considered him as a son.

Amelia now lives with her grandfather and two local boys who tend the cows. Her father and brother were shot by the Civil Guard, and her mother died of grief. Her sister is married and lives in Barcelona. She weeps in Francisco's arms, composes herself, and warns him that the Civil Guard is always about: they store barbed wire inside the barn, she gives as an example, wire which they unroll in the hills to keep escapees from reaching France. She begs for him to stay until the snow thaws, but he argues that the snow is their protection as few enemy patrols dare face the brutal winter.

Francisco whistles for his comrades, who rise from hiding and approach the farmhouse, glad to get out of the cold. Amelia warms leftover stew, offers wine, and cuts their hair. For the next three days, they sleep in the cellar on sweet-smelling hay, gaining strength to climb the snowy mountains. Amelia prepares food for their journey—boiled potatoes, bread, and sausages, bits of chocolate wrapped in newspaper. Francisco leaves Amelia with ten thousand pesetas. She is crying when he and his comrades disappear among the trees.

The band of guerrillas returns to the mountains where Francisco first practiced rock climbing and learned to handle explosives. They follow the railroad tracks toward Puigcerda and avoid Olot, which bustles with enemy soldiers. They come upon a large shed flanked by rolls of barbed wire, unguarded. Inside, Francisco and Mier are greeted by a framed picture of Franco on the wall. They spit in the direction of the picture.

Francisco decides to create a diversion. They splash oil, gasoline, and paint throughout the shed. Francisco next lights a slow fuse attached to sticks of dynamite, and then they run in the direction of the railroad. They stop and look back when an explosion lights up the sky. Within half an hour, troops from the nearby military post come running.

Francisco and his comrades watch as the shed crackles and

blazes. When they hear the rhythm of marching boot steps, they withdraw from the road to higher ground and quickly set up an ambush. When the enemy is a few yards away, they jump out from behind boulders and shoot seven dead, then rush uphill into a treeless, snowy terrain. They march through the cold, sometimes stopping to huddle together for warmth. At dawn, through binoculars, Francisco observes Nationalist soldiers and Civil Guardsmen swarming below. His attention is then drawn skyward. A low-flying plane skims some trees and circles twice before strafing wanderers on a path below. After the plane flies away, Francisco and his comrades scramble down to the path. They find two dead civilians and a wounded man, Luis Quamara, who tells them that he and his comrades had been on their way to France.

Francisco dresses the man's wounds. A political commissar from Granada, Luis is gaunt from hunger and has no option but to join them. They give their new comrade bread and a single sausage, which he devours in front of them. They climb the rocky side of a mountain and soon make out a distant lake. It has begun to snow, and the wind howls through the trees. They walk in the direction of the lake; after two hours, they stand at its shores. They continue their journey by next passing through woods so thick that the sky is nearly eclipsed. In the late afternoon, they manage to bring down a doe, which they skin and roast.

They carry on for another freezing day then realize—to their surprise and self-anger—that they have been walking in a circle! They camp in a cave near Olot and start again in the morning. A mile into the day's trek they are greeted by a civilian dressed in rags and wearing bad shoes. Unshaven and dirty, the stranger informs them in Castilian that his name is Marquez Sanchez Olivar and that he's trying to get to France. Francisco remains suspicious, even when he shows his identification papers. The man talks too much.

When the stranger claims that his aunt lives in Olot, Francisco leaves the two new additions with Mier and Melchol and goes with Antonio to inquire. He locates the aunt's house. When she answers the door, he begs her not be scared, that he and his comrade are only there to inquire about her nephew. She regards Francisco without worry even after he admits that he's a former Republican soldier and that he and Antonio are trying to get to France. She invites the men inside, where an old man and a girl of ten sit at a table. She takes her guests to the kitchen, feeds them bread, black sausage, and cheese, then fills their canteens with wine. Francisco spies a photo on the wall: Olivar in a Falangist uniform. The old man notices Francisco's interest in the photo. He laments with a sigh that his nephew is a bad man who informs on persons trying to cross into France. He even had *him*—his own uncle—put in a concentration camp. The family is scared of Olivar, but what are they to do?

Francisco has heard enough. He and Antonio return to their cave. Neither says anything to Mier or Melchor about what they have learned. The next day they come to a bridge. After many minutes of observation, they cross safely and continue to a small farm occupied by an old woman and an old man, along with three children. Their livelihood is raising rabbits. The family invites them to a meager dinner of potatoes and chestnuts. The old man tells Francisco of the comings and goings of the Civil Guardsmen; earlier in the day he observed them leading three prisoners away. The old man cautions them to be careful. The guard post is at the end of the road.

That evening, after a few hours of sleep, Francisco shakes Olivar awake and tells him that it's his turn to act as sentinel. When Melchor comes in from the cold, Olivar shrugs into his jacket and goes out to assume his duty as guard. Francisco watches from a window, then slips out of the house and waits on the path to the village. Francisco is sure the traitor has plans to inform the Civil Guard of their whereabouts. A few minutes later Olivar appears hustling down the path. Francisco steps out from hiding and plunges a knife into his heart, then rakes it against his throat. Olivar falls with blood spurting from his throat. Francisco writes "This is how traitors die" on a piece of paper and places the message on Olivar's chest, weighted with a rock. The enemy will recognize the work of *El Mexicano*.

Francisco returns to the farm and gives his comrades details of what has taken place. Next, he tells them that they will attack the guard post and release prisoners held there. He strangles two rabbits, stuffs them wrapped in paper in his rucksack, and places a thousand pesetas on the table. The five of them set out for the post. The attack is simple and direct: several Civil Guardsmen are asleep at a table when grenades crash through the window. Mier and Mechol follow up with gunfire. The lieutenant is shot behind his desk and three guardsmen are killed on the second floor.

The men release four prisoners from a locked room then hear a burst of gunfire below. Francisco goes outside. Luis, the political commissar, has shot a guardsman who had leaped from a window and was trying to run away. Luis is jubilant. In all, they have killed nine guardsmen and captured two tommy guns and thirty grenades.

Three of the four prisoners choose to join them. The new recruits are Catalans: Ruissol, Castel, and the youngest, Malaguez, who is acquainted with the region. Francisco feels certain that none is a traitor. Malaguez says that the border is only twenty-five miles away, but warns them that the Aras Pass is likely patrolled by Civil Guardsmen. He suggests that they go by way of Puigcerda, a three-day trek. They set off and follow the railroad tracks. A few miles from the guard post, Francisco regrets not taking any provisions—Luis's first kill had distracted him. So he teaches his men to eat roots. And when they come upon a boar, they kill it, roast it, and eat it to the bone.

On the third day the men descend into a valley and cross a set of abandoned railroad tracks. They take refuge in a charcoal maker's hut. The next morning Francisco observes a column of enemy soldiers. He tells his men to prepare to decamp, for he is certain that the soldiers are on their trail. They have been fleeing over snow-covered ground, where their boot prints make easy markers for the guardsmen to track. Francisco looks back often, a finger on the trigger of his tommy gun. A snap of tree limbs or a sudden flight of birds keeps him alert. At nightfall they camp under some trees, not daring to light a fire.

Without explanation Francisco leaves his men and retraces their steps in the snow by the light of the moon. Soon he comes upon a large fire. He crawls on his belly and counts sixteen soldiers, with six Civil Guardsmen acting as sentinels. Two machine guns have been set up, but no one is manning them. The soldiers are talkative and full of laughter, their faces red before the campfire. They are singing an Andalusian song and one man is dancing.

Francisco would kill the Civil Guardsmen without a worrisome thought, but the regular soldiers, to his mind, are poverty-stricken draftees, not Fascist volunteers. He carefully returns to camp and sleeps there in the cold. In the morning, the enemy patrol has vanished. Francisco's men scavenge what is left behind: a few potatoes and a sack of carob beans. They eat them before they set off into the forest. Soon they come upon a village that Malaguez recognizes as a place where smugglers operate. They stop at a large house where the owner, a quiet merchant, has many things on the shelves, none marked with a price but all obviously for sale.

After Francisco buys provisions, the owner takes him to a second-floor window and points out a road that climbs Puerto de Tosas, a mountain that rises six thousand feet. The owner advises against that route, as it is defended by concrete bunkers armed with machine guns. The passes are also guarded and the winter weather will be a concern. He suggests another route through a series of ridges.

Francisco and his men remain three days and nights in the village, devouring large quantities of food to bolster their strength. Then they load their rucksacks and embark on what will be a twenty-five-mile trek through perilous terrain. While it is painfully cold to walk in the snow, they find delight in the wild goats with long beards. Every rocky perch seems to host one of these goats chewing his cud and watching, with apparent curiosity, these struggling men pass. As they climb, the wild goats are replaced by chamois, smaller animals with short horns. Unlike the goats, the chamois shy away when the men come near to pet them.

Then a blizzard overwhelms them. They can't see more than ten feet and their hands and feet begin to freeze. Francisco orders a halt. They huddle under blankets and wait out the storm. Two days pass. On the morning of the third day, Francisco tries to shake his comrades awake. But Mechol and Ruissol have died from the cold, and Luis's feet are frozen and blue. Francisco makes a stretcher from branches; the remaining men place Luis on it and take turns carrying him.

They come to a large farm where the farmer welcomes them, feeds them, and throws more logs onto the fire. The men sleep in the barn, using the cows for warmth. They depart after three days of rest, with Luis still in a stretcher, and follow the railroad tracks. It's not long before they are freezing again. They march a mile then rest huddled together against the cold. They build a fire to warm their feet, continue to march for a time, then stop and build another fire. They are looking for a way up an embankment when they are hit by tommy guns and grenades. Castel, Mier, and Malaguez are killed at once; Luis is shot as he tries to rise from his stretcher.

Francisco drops to the ground and manages to roll away from the flying bullets. Only he and Antonio remain. The two crouch against a pile of rocks, then rise and run ploddingly through the deep snow. They have lost their tommy guns, but Francisco still has a pistol, an extra clip of bullets, and two grenades. Antonio's pistol is empty.

Snow is falling heavily. The two men pause behind a bush as they catch their breath. Antonio is bleeding from a shoulder wound. They wait for the enemy to creep forward. Francisco hands Antonio his extra clip and one grenade. Soon four Civil Guardsmen appear, trudging through the deep snow toward them. Francisco stands and with all his strength tosses his grenade. Antonio throws his next. After the explosion, they both fire on the guardsmen. The snow is red with blood.

They recover a tommy gun from the dead, along with some clips of bullets and two grenades, then hobble toward and through a tunnel. Antonio can't keep up. He stops and bends over, his blood dotting the snow. Francisco pulls on Antonio's arm as he begs him not to give up, reminding him that they are almost there. They trudge onward, each step thigh-deep in snow. A few feet separate them, then a few yards. Francisco turns and pleads for Antonio not to give up.

Francisco remembers the old man's instruction: after the tunnel, they should climb straight ahead. He climbs halfway up an embankment, then turns and calls for Antonio through the falling snow. He calls a third and a fourth time, but Antonio does not reply. The world around him is entirely white and the wind has torn off his hat. Francisco stumbles into a crevasse and sinks to his chest into the snow. He believes that he is dying when he hears a voice calling. Through nearly closed eyes, he sees a blur of a man descending a rope. The rescuer reaches him and ties the rope around him. Above the crevasse, two other men begin to pull.

Francisco is carried to a house, stripped of his wet clothes, and placed in front of the fire. One of the men slowly drips hot water on his body, then cold water. They raise him into a sitting position, give his body a brisk rubbing, and then wrap him in heated blankets. Francisco is unable to speak. He stays in front of the fire for three days.

The blizzard continues. Antonio, his last comrade, is buried in the snow. From a makeshift bed, Francisco watches his rescuers sort corn and play games to stave off the boredom of winter days. They eat the same meal every day: potatoes, chickpeas, and beans with chunks of pork. The master of the house pours out glasses of wine—large ones for the men, smaller ones for the women. They throw their excrement out the window—and quickly—because of the howling wind. One of the women tells Francisco that it was while doing this chore she heard his screams for help.

One night Francisco brings out a block of cigarette papers and, at the kitchen table, begins to make notes about his years as a soldier. Fascinated, the family hovers around him; they do not know how to read or write. Francisco decides to teach the children the alphabet. He hangs a leather apron on the wall and uses charcoal to write letters on this makeshift blackboard. The first word they learn to write is "mama." The adults join in. The first word they learn to write is also "mama."

Francisco stays fifteen days with his rescuers. He aches to move on, and tells them so. The master of the house returns Francisco's pistol, bullets, and grenades, then packs his rucksack with bread, sausages, ham, and two onions. Francisco gives the master all of his remaining pesetas—forty-two thousand. He will have no more use for Spanish currency.

He departs with a young man, who has grown tired of mountain life. He is eager to see the outside world and happy for a new adventure—he is sixteen years old. The journey is short, almost too short, and saddens Francisco as he remembers Antonio, who was only a day away from the border. In spring his body may be found and properly buried.

Francisco and the young man cross a frozen river, descend briefly into a valley, and then up a snowy peak bright with wintry sunlight. Within a few hours they are in a village on the French side. Francisco leads the way to a bakery and informs the woman behind the counter that he is an escapee from a Spanish prison. He hands over his weapons and takes off his Legionnaire's coat. The woman has the calm look of someone who has seen all this before. She doesn't ask for details, but seems to understand his plight. She disappears into a back room and returns with a set of old clothes. Francisco goes into another room to change. When he comes out, he casts a glance in the mirror over the counter—he sees that he has aged. The woman gives him three thousand francs. Then she leads the two men outside and points to the main road into France.

Where to go but Arles, his hometown. Francisco will see his mother and grandmother. He will live another kind of life, he is certain. He will sleep, find work, and be home, always at home. He is twenty-four-years old with scars on almost every part of his body. Little does he know that within a year's time he will join the French Resistance against Hitler and Nazi Germany. Justice, he will believe all his life, must prevail.

Who's Who

Friends   Enemies

Friends	Enemies
Republican Army	*Nationalist Army*
Lister Corps	*Carlists*
International Bridgades	*Civil Guardsmen*
	Moroccans from the Spanish Protectorate
	Red Berets
	Legionaries (Spanish Foreign Legion)
	German and Italian soldiers

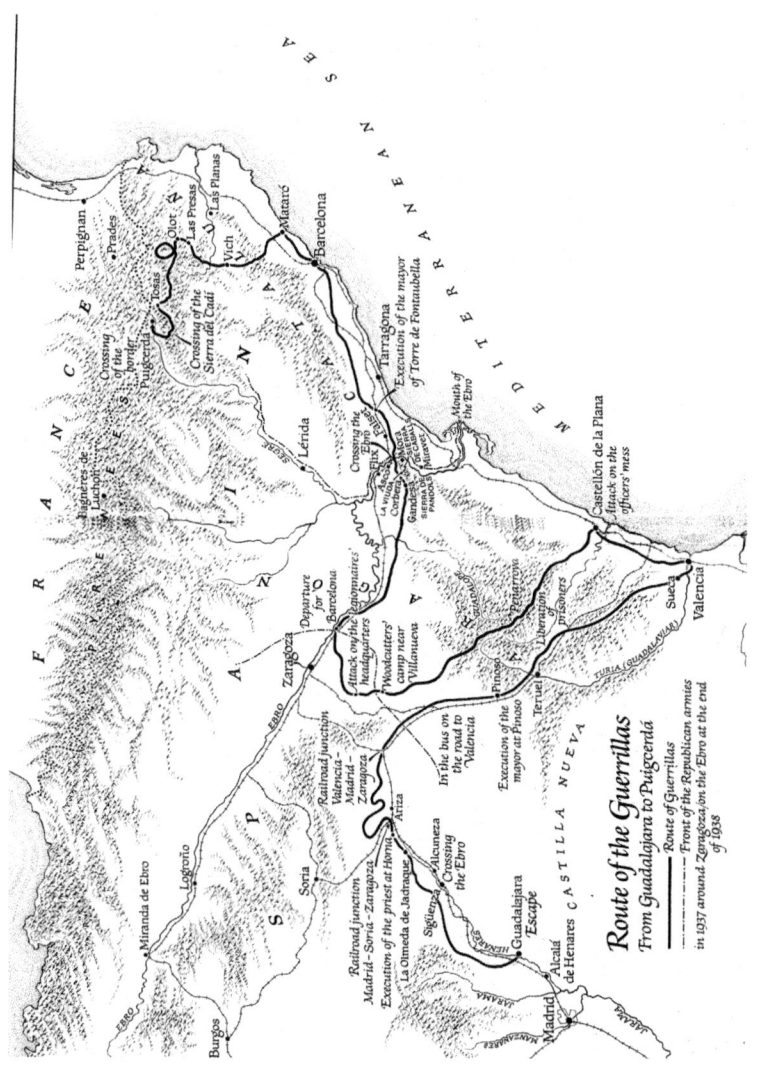

Route of the Guerrillas
From Guadalajara to Puigcerdá

GARY SOTO is author of many collections of poetry, essays, plays, including *Sudden Loss of Dignity* and *The Spark and Fire of It: A Romance*, both available from Stephen F. Austin State University Press. The Gary Soto Literary Museum is located at Fresno City College, where he began writing in the early 1970s. He lives in Berkeley, California.

CPSIA information can be obtained
at www.ICGtesting.com
Printed in the USA
FSHW04n1622060418
46614FS

9 781622 881635